HISTORY *in* PLAIN SIGHT

about

ABOUT JOAQUIN MILLER, AMBROSE BIERCE, AND THE REAL BLACK BART

Margaret Guilford-Kardell

ARCHWAY PUBLISHING

Archway Publishing books may be ordered through booksellers or by contacting:

Archway Publishing
1663 Liberty Drive
Bloomington, IN 47403
www.archwaypublishing.com
1 (888) 242-5904

Because of the dynamic nature of the Internet, any web addresses or links contained in this book may have changed since publication and may no longer be valid. The views expressed in this work are solely those of the author and do not necessarily reflect the views of the publisher, and the publisher hereby disclaims any responsibility for them.

Any people depicted in stock imagery provided by Thinkstock are models, and such images are being used for illustrative purposes only.
Certain stock imagery © Thinkstock.

ISBN: 978-1-4808-4424-7 (sc)
ISBN: 978-1-4808-4425-4 (e)

Library of Congress Control Number: 2017903055

Print information available on the last page.

Archway Publishing rev. date: 8/15/2017

I thank God for the extended time given me to be able to
dedicate this book to future historians on their quest for truth.

Contents

Foreword vii

Preface viii

Acknowledgement x

Introduction xiii

Chapter 1   In Todays World 1

Chapter 2   Joaquin Miller and Alvy Boles 9

Chapter 3   Their Idaho Days 13

Chapter 4   The Asbills 26

Chapter 5   The Miller/Boles Connection 30

Chapter 6   After the Massacre 35

Chapter 7   Alvy Boles in Yreka 40

Chapter 8   From Trails to Stage Roads 47

Chapter 9   Gold Mining 53

Chapter 10 "More Clewes" 57

Chapter 11 Miller Returns 66

Chapter 12 The Alva (Alvy) Boles Family 69

Chapter 13 The London Celebrity Returns and Black Bart's
Celebrity Begins...73

Chapter 14 Black Bard becomes Black Bart 75

Chapter 15 History Coalesces 80

Chapter 16 Robbery No. 3 86

Chapter 17 The Reader Ranch 88

Chapter 18 Homeward Bound 90
Chapter 19 An Expensive Year 92
Chapter 20 1879 Back to Butte Co. and Shasta Co.........................94
Chapter 21 Back in Sonoma Co. 97
Chapter 22 Robberies No. 20-28 105
Chapter 23 Bart's Last Robbery...113
Chapter 24 Capture 114
Chapter 25 Confession/Confusion 116
Chapter 26 Recognition 118
Chapter 27 San Quentin 121
Chapter 28 Bart's Life After Prison 130
Chapter 29 What Bart Says.. 137
Chapter 30 Douglas Co. Nevada 158
Chapter 31 Retrospection 160

Epilogue 166
Appendix... 173
    The Lost Cabin.. 173
    Old Boles's Story 174
    Late In the Summer 175
    An Exploring Tour 177
    The Grizzly and the Gold 178
    Building the Cabin... 180
    The Cabin Lost 181
Bibliography of Margaret Guilford-Kardell's Research 183
About the Author 193

Therto have I a remedie in my thoght,
　By a clewe of twyn as he hath gon.
　The same weye he may return a-non,
　Folowynge alwey the thred as he hath come.

Geoffrey Chaucer. *The Legend of Ariadne*, Part VI of
The Legend of Good Women. ca. 1388

Foreword

Alan Rosenus in 2016 wrote "Margaret Kardell continues to uncover intriguing material about some of the West's most colorful figures."

Preface

Last night's May 10, 2015 T.V. airing of Bill O'Reilly's *Legends and Lies* of the West featured the life and times of C.E. Boles as California's most famous stage robber 1875- 1883. It drew mainly from the *2009 Black Bart: The Poet Bandit* by Gail Jenner, an award winning Siskiyou Co. novelist and Lou Legerton a V.P. Marketing Specialist for Wells Fargo.

Jenner and Legerton followed a long line of books and articles that parroted newspaper reports and speculations about the robberies after each occurrence. All seemed ignorant of local history and none, except Collins and Levene paid attention to the four quadrants in which the robberies took place which gave me my first clue as to real identity of the Real Black Bart.

At the 2013 Mt. Shasta Sisson Shasta Museum for their "A Man and the Mountain" celebration of the life of Joaquin Miller (1839-1913). I was lead presenter there and I shared the results of my research over the past 43 years.

Joaquin Miller and his friend Black Bart were two of the most colorful, most often misunderstood, but most often celebrated figures from California's Gold Rush days. Both traveled the same trails. But Miller became a Celebrity poet, author, lawyer, and journalist while Black Bart became California's most celebrated stage robber.

The best researched *Black Bart* robbery records were presented by William Collins and Bruce Levene. Their 1992 second edition was used as the basis for the robbery information herein following.

Yes, Black Bart's true identity has always been speculative. But now, thanks to the U.S. Census, Google, and my research we have his real story and the stories of the friends he made along the way.

Acknowledgement

First to God for giving me the time to finish this manuscript.

Next my Father, Frank I. Guilford whose civil war father was an avid Joaquin Miller reader. My father told me tales of the Chris Evans and Sontag robberies as we traveled the San Joaquin Valley, starting my interest in our California history. Later in life my father was involved with the Oakland Lions club, and the Boys Club Camp on Matquaw Flats where Joaquin Miller was captured after his escape from jail.

To my husband, John R. Kardell for my experiences and travel around the world beginning with my experiences in Shasta County where I began my Indian studies. He surveyed the Oakland Boys Club property for them and at which time my father bought adjoining property to protect the Boys Club entrance. We later bought this property from my father and built our retirement home there from which we could see the trails Joaquin Miller had traveled. We then became acquainted with our Indian neighbors.

Local historians, Helen Hogue, who introduced me to the Historical Society in Redding and started me on my Indian research. Their first President Mae Hazel Southern. I read how in her unpublished (later stolen) memoirs how she identified Black Bart.

And to Jim Dotta, the Archaeologist who introduced me to many Indians and with whom I wrote "Occasional Papers of the Redding

Museum Paper No.1". Next his friend Joe Mazzini who was my computer operator and fellow historian on Genealogical papers and Miller research.

Jim Simas, born and raised in Scott Valley, who gifted me "History of Siskiyou County, California" by Harry L. Wells 1881. Which started providing "clewe's" as my work on the history of Joaquin Miller and the Wintu Indians on the McCloud River area progressed. Eventually leading to this book.

Archeologist with the United States Forest Service Julie Cassidy with whom I visited many historical sites along the McCloud River area.

Glennys Christie my editor in later years who helped me get many Joaquin Miller booklets and my Joaquin Miller newsletter published. She typed and edited the Joaquin Miller Bibliography on-line.

Scott McKeown for financial support of Joaquin Miller Bibliography.

Rick Miller A.K.A. Mendicino Rick, for his help to identify people in photos, as weil as his passionate recollections of Mendicino Co area history.

Arlene Zornes also from Mendocino Co. granddaughter of Nat Smith, told us where he lived at various times and also his later trade route from Fort Bragg to Ukiah via trails and roads that Black Bart could have used as well.

Bruce Levene has B.A. in American Civilization from the University of Iowa, with graduate work in history. He has taught at College of the Redwoods in Fort Bragg. He has written for various publications, and authored, edited, and compiled numerous books on California history, primarily about Mendocino County. For his 1992 Black Bart which best laid out the geography of the robberies thus inadvertently and unknowingly nailing the identity of Alvy

Boles as Black Bart from the stories told of and by those people involved. Bruce Levene's maps, pictures and research were exhaustively thorough.

Eric Vollmers & Melinda Salisbury research associates for Humboldt State University Cultural Resources Facility. Together they prepared a visual presentation which accompanied my speech in 2013, visually bringing the whole story together.

I also need to acknowledge descendants of those who were related to or knew Alvy Boles who started coming forward as they learned of my work: first was David Lee Boles, Great, Great Grandson of Alvy Boles; second was Jill Kane Great, Great Granddaughter of Frank Asbill and Linda Markham Curry, Great Grandniece of Edward Markham. Ed Clouet provided information about Dorcas Boles Gordon.

Johnny Ford for helping take care of my property, moving, and building many of the shelving units to hold my research.

Will Petty III since my relocating to Washington State, as my caregiver, sounding board, and proof reader. Reading to me as eyesight is failing.

Cory Dodge without whose patience and help typing, editing, and proofing this book, would never have come to fruition.

Introduction

Indiana people were typical of the sense of civility and integrity in relationships in those early days which were carried west to the goldfields. The relationships of the miners and their family and friends was paramount as they lived out their lives in their new locations in Shasta and Siskiyou Counties. These characteristics were common to the Masons, Oddfellows, Eclampus Vitus, and other such organizations which provided the leaders in all the communities.

This was proven to me early on when Jimmy Simas gave me a copy of "History of Siskiyou County, California" By Harry L. Wells 1881. Because Jimmy remembered his grandmother, a Davidson, telling him stories on the steps of the Jerimiah Davidson home in Scott Valley, about Joaquin Miller and Black Bart. Where later in this same Davidson's house the 1860 census records Black Bart's oldest son living while he was growing up.

The Davidson's had come through Oregon City in 1852 just as the Miller's had previously.

In 1852 Jeremiah Davidson, was in the Humbug area when *"Frenchy Whipped on Scott River"* account occurred. And undoubtedly later was in Yreka when A. Boles signed the arrest warrant for Dr. Baid. *To any constable on Shasta Plains Township this day complaint having laid before me the Vigilant Committee that the crime of felony has Ben committed and accusing the above named Dr. Baid of the same therefore you are to arrest the said Dr. Baid and bring him before the people to be dealt with according to their judgement. A. Boles, Chairman Committee, Yreka, 1852.* (Wells 1881, 104,105)

This is the same A Boles that is photographed in his blacksmith shop in Rocky Bar, Idaho in 1864. Joaquin Miller as "Esmeralda" wrote in the Boise News, October 15, 1864 pg.2 col 4, how Boles and Annibal were blacksmiths in Rocky Bar, Idaho.

Today's 2016 culture will not understand the culture of CA in 1883 when Boles was captured. People in 1883 didn't go out of their way to drag a families name through the mud, especially someone they all liked. Just last week a modern historian exploded in disbelief when I was trying to explain to him that nobody revealed the name of Black Bart when his picture appeared in the newspaper at the time of his capture. His response was that he "didn't believe nobody did that." My reply was "There was no more reward offered by Wells Fargo at the time he was in custody. No one had been hurt. No one had money stolen from them, except Wells Fargo, and Black Bart had led Wells Fargo to the cache from his last robbery, which reduced his sentence. And a citizen had remarked "if he saw a stage being robbed he would walk the other way."

Joaquin Miller and Edward Markham's work and family histories gave me my first "clewe's" to the real story of Black Bart and Alvy Boles. But Joaquin Miller would not have connected Black Bart to Alvy Boles in 1873.

As you read *History in Plain Sight* enjoy these revelations which will help us better understand our past, our ancestors, their neighbors, and their culture.

Margaret Guilford-Kardell

Chapter 1

In Todays World

In the year 2015 Bill O'Reilly produced a documentary accurately called "Legends and Lies of the Far West". One episode was about Black Bart as portrayed by the paper at the time of his robberies in California from 1875-1883 and continued by creative journalists from that time on. But none of them were about the real Black Bart.

The first acknowledgement of Black Bart's true identity came from H.L.W. in an 1888 newspaper paragraph, validating that Joaquin Miller had received his first minig tip from Alvy Boles. Another major indication was in 1916 San Diego Fair when Edwin Markham told his story of having met the real Black Bart as a pack train operator in Mendocino Co. CA. when Markham, as a boy was herding sheep.

In 1883, Markham, like everyone else, had recognized Black Bart from his picture in the paper when he was arrested. But, probably to keep the reputation of his family from damaging publicity, everybody went along with the name by which he was arrested.

Black Bart arrest photo 1883

My first "clewe" to Black Bart's identity came from my studying the life of Joaquin Miller. This began when my third grade teacher (not seventh grade as they do today) in Oakland, CA introduced us to his poem *"Columbus"*.

Columbus

Behind him lay the gray Azores,
Behind the Gates of Hercules;
Before him not the ghost of shores,
Before him only shoreless seas.
The good mate said: "Now we must pray,
For lo! The very stars are gone.
Brave Admiral, speak, what shall I say?"
"Why, say, 'Sail on! Sail on! And on!'"

"My men grow mutinous day by day;
My men grow ghastly wan and weak."
The stout mate thought of home; a spray
Of salt wave washed his swarthy cheek.

"What shall I say, brave Admiral, say,
If we sight naught but seas at dawn?"
"Why, you shall say at break of day,
'Sail on! Sail on! And on!'"

They sailed and sailed, as winds might blow,
Until at last the blanched mate said:
"Why, now not even God would know
Should I and all my men fall dead.
These very winds forget their way,
For God from these dead seas is gone.
Now speak, brave Admiral, speak and say" --
He said, "Sail on! Sail on! And on!"

They sailed. They sailed. Then spake the mate:
"This mad sea shows his teeth tonight.
He curls his lip, he lies in wait,
With lifted teeth, as if to bite!
Brave Admiral, say but one good word:
What shall we do when hope is gone?"
The words leapt like a leaping sword:
"Sail on! Sail on! Sail on! And on!"

Then pale and worn, he kept his deck,
And peered through darkness. Ah, that night
Of all dark nights! And then a speck --
A light! A light! At last a light!
It grew, a starlit flag unfurled!
It grew to be Time's burst of dawn.
He gained a world; he gave that world
Its grandest lesson: "On! Sail on!"
Joaquin Miller

We read the poem aloud in class and were each asked to see if we could write a better poem. Some did!

Next in my Junior High School days my cousin and I hiked from my home in the hills over to Joaquin Miller's "Hights," now Joaquin Miller Park, where Girl Scouts used to meet and roast marshmallows.

My next connection with Miller was in the early 1950's when my engineering husband was working in Redding CA. While shopping in Safeway I made friends with Jim Simas as we were both interested in Shasta Co. history and I had mentioned Miller, famous for having been in jail in Old Shasta for allegedly stealing a horse. Jim said I should be studying Siskiyou Co. as Miller had really been there first.

Jim remembered sitting on his Davidson grandmother's front porch in Scott Valley and hearing her tell stories about Joaquin Miller and Black Bart. But he had forgotten them, so one day he gifted me Harry L. Wells *History of Siskiyou County, California 1881*.

When Wells published his book he was jealous of the success of Joaquin Miller's 1873 novel *Life Amongst the Modocs*. Miller had capitalized on the world-wide publicity of the Modoc War to launch his own story and that of an unknown group of Indians called the *Wintu.*

Doubly frustrating to Wells was the public's daily interest in the stage robber Black Bart, rather than history. Little did Wells realize that Black Bart had been a source of many of the stories he himself had just published. And Wells, who never once mentioned the *Wintu,* probably thought, like everyone else, that Miller had really been writing about the Modocs, when actually he was writing about the *Wintu,* who were also a part of the history of Siskiyou Co. when it was originally a part of Shasta Co.

Strangely enough, from Wells' own work and sources he

overlooked, came our first "clewe"s to the true story about Joaquin Miller and the Real Black Bart. It was Wells who, when listing other robbers in his *History of Siskiyou County, California 1881* referred to him in print as the mysterious "Black Bard." (Wells 1881, 166)

And it was Harry L. Wells, b. in Illinois in 1854, who in 1881 first accurately accused Miller of having taken factual occurrences in Siskiyou Co. and making them into his own life story in his so-called autobiographical novel, *Life Amongst the Modocs.*

Actually, writing under his own name, Cincinnatus H. Miller, in the *Daily Alta Californian* at age 15, Miller had written; not of having walked to California with a young friend, but of having come down from Oregon on the steamer *Peytonia* most probably with his eldest brother, John D. born in 1837, and whose birth date he sometimes appropriated. (*Daily Alta California* Vol.5, No. 254, 13 Sept. 1854)

Miller wrote that piece August 26, 1854 at Deer Creek, *Umpqua* Valley, today's Roseburg, Oregon. He wrote very well about having traveled inland from Crescent City, California over the coast range of mountains to where he was staying with the postmaster. Perhaps his brother was with their family friends the Applegates. Miller's letter to the editor indicated he would be sending on more such epistles when he reached the California mines. But that didn't work out until years later. In 1854 Joaquin Miller and his brother, John D., started their journey into the gold rush world by walking from Crescent City, CA to Roseburg, OR. Then they pushed on to Jacksonville, OR to join other Oregon miners and then down into California to a golden future.

Miller never wrote again about traveling with his brother or their being in the mines together until John D. died, in the 1870's. Then he only wrote their times in the Idaho mines in the 1860's. Only then did Miller reference their having been in the Siskiyou's in the 1850's and his brother being called "Wabash", because they were originally from Indiana.

They weren't among strangers in Yreka for many other recently minted Oregonians were there too, like the Davidsons.

Some miners were led into Siskiyou Co. by Oregon's Governor Lane. Govenor Lane (or his son) whom historians say had gone to school under Hulings Miller, Joaquin's father.

But in 1854 young fifteen year old Cincinnatus H. Miller, on his first job as cook and errand boy for other miners, wasn't writing about the past but penning "Letters to the Editors" of local papers which did not publish them, and keeping a journal which eventually did get published, posthumously.

Miller was meeting everyone, making friends, and mentally storing away experiences that would make him one of the most colorful historians of the Gold Rush days.

Most precious to him was Mary St Clair, queen of Yreka's 1854 *demi monde*, who had paid Miller twenty dollars to recite Carol Norton's poem. Which ended with the oft repeated signature line by a lonely soldier singing about longing to return home to "Bingen on the Rhine". This was at a welcome home party for Sid Oldham at Yreka's American Hotel and was the beginning of Miller's career as a celebrity. But Miller never wrote about her until an article in (Ambrose Bierce's) *The Wasp* in 1891. Although she was a trusted confidant and friend through Miller's Walla Walla, WA and Canyon City, OR days. She had saloons in both places and Miller continued to value her opinions long after his wife, Minnie Myrtle, forbade him to have conversations with any women when they were all living in Canyon City.

Another young performer in Yreka in the 1850's was Lotta Crabtree at the Arcade saloon. She was somewhere between 7-12 years of age and thus the Shirley Temple of her day. To the delight of the miners and her mother who gathered in her apron the gold coins tossed on the stage.

In later writings Miller would also tell of having seen John Heenan fight in Yreka. And in the 1870's when Miller and his wife Minnie, were first in San Francisco he wrote of having become a very close friend with Adah Isaacs Menken, Heenan's wife. Adah was then riding her horse on stage in "Mazeppa". Menken is now referred to as the "first celebrity actress."

Miller had arrived in Yreka after the summer fire of 1854 so there was probably lots of rebuilding going on. He probably heard of the "street murder" committed by Jakey Williams in a town of around 5,000, when in 1849 Yreka had only been flat pasture land.

Yreka had to have been a truly exciting place for a boy of 15. Miller soon met many miners and others who would become the story tellers or characters in Miller's own outpourings of poems, articles, books, and plays written during his lifetime.

It was years later in the 1890's when he began to write about his days in the mines of Idaho, late 1860 to1864. He began to reminisce about the miners he and his brother John D. had first known in Yreka and with whom they were again mining with in Idaho.

John D.'s closest friend from those first Yreka days was Peter Bablaine whom Miller immortalized as "Old Baboon" and who, like Black Bart, was the inspiration for the poem with which this book will close.

In prose Miller wrote about some prostitutes, or shall we say "ladies of the evening," or as Miller wrote "fallen angels" who called upon an ailing elderly miner, "Old Baboon". Whom perhaps these "ladies" too had known in earlier Yreka days:

> They gave him gifts, and money, and above all, words
> of encouragement and kindness. He received it all in

silence; but I saw when they had gone that the coldness of his face had tempered down, like a wintry hillside under a day of sun. He moodily filled the meerschaum they had brought him, and after driving a volume of smoke through his nose, looked quietly at me and said: `Society is wrong. These women are not bad women. For my part, I begin to find so much that is evil in that which the world calls good, and so much that is good in what the world calls evil, that I refuse to draw a distinction where God has not.' then he fired a double-barreled volley at society through his nose, and throwing out volume after volume of smoke as a sort of redoubt between himself and the world he hated, drifted silently into a tropical golden land of dreams (Miller 1968: 4).

Chapter 2
Joaquin Miller and Alvy Boles

In his 1873 *Life Amongst the Modocs.* Miller wrote only of being befriended in Yreka by a Black Nicaraguan who tended the stable in Yreka. Miller didn't write about Alvy Boles until his first mention of him in a news clip about Rocky Bar, Idaho in 1864. And not again until 1883 when he wrote of Alvy Boles having been his friend since his own first days in Yreka in 1854.

Meanwhile, obviously Alvy Boles had been the source of many of Miller's stories. Miller's version of Alvy Boles's the "Lost Cabin Mine" surfaced around when Miller published his *Songs of the Sierras* in Boston. In a July 27, 1871 review in New York's *Evening Post* p.2, cols. 4, 5 there appeared a copy of a letter from the English critic George Francis Armstrong.

And another letter which included the story of the "Lost Cabin Mine" as told to an unidentified writer by Joaquin Miller in England in 1870/71:

> I first saw Miller in the mountains of Northern California, in 1854. He was a mere boy, and could not have been more than thirteen or fourteen years of age [15]. He was with an old man called `Mountain Joe,' who had been one of Frémont's guides and who treated him as his own boy. He had taught him the use of the pistol,

with which he afterwards made himself famous in that country. Miller's home was somewhere in Oregon Territory [near Coburg, north of Eugene], and it was said he had run away from it. The summer following [June of 1855] Mountain Joe led a party of miners against the Indians, and in the fight which ensued, Miller was shot in the face with an arrow, and nearly lost his life. Not long after he originated with Mountain Joe and McDougal, the great gold excitement known as 'The Lost Cabin,' which many Californians will remember with regret.

This McDougal was a famous character. He was the brother of Governor McDougal [1851] of California, one of the finest looking men in the mountains, and known in the country as `Prince George'. Whether the `Lost Cabin' was reality or myth, and there are many who believe it was not all a myth, the company always had bags of gold-dust, although they were never seen to be engaged in mining. They rode the finest horses, were armed with the choicest weapons, and wore the most splendid accoutrements; `Prince George' especially being noted for the magnificence of his dress. Every few months they would `drop down' to San Francisco, put up at the best hotels, and attract the attention of the whole town by their lavish expenditure of money. Then as suddenly as they came, they disappeared, and all attempts to follow them or trace the sources of their wealth, were utterly futile. In time the Lost Cabiners disappeared, and it was said they had joined the filibuster Walker in Mexico [Nicaragua]. McDougal never returned, and it is believed that he is at this moment a chief of the

Patagonians; and all traces of `Mountain Joe' has been lost. ("Joaquin Miller" *The Evening Post* (New York) vol. 70 (Thursday July 27, 1871): 2: 4, 5.) [Published by William C. Bryant & Co.]

Our Appendix version of the "Lost Cabin Mine" story was written by H. L.W. [Harry L. Wells] referenced in Wells's book. (Wells 1881, 116). It is thus obvious that Harry L. Wells and Joaquin Miller both obtained this same "Lost Cabin Stories" from Alvy Boles, whom they both knew in the Siskiyou area. But they published the story at different times.

Thomas Penfield's 1971 *Directory of Buried Treasure, P.*39 lists not the "Lost Cabin Mine" but Alvy Boles (Lost Mine). Here it gives the area reference as Shasta City, Shasta Co. suffice it to say that people were confused as to where this "Lost Cabin" might be and Oregon's Crater Lake was first found by miners while looking for this same Lost Cabin mine.

And census records only further confuse the real history between Wells, Miller, and Boles. Harry L. Wells, the historian was evidently born in Illinois in 1854 while another Harry L. Wells born in 1856 in Wisconsin was in Butteville [Edgewood], Siskiyou Co. with his father Hudson Wells in 1860. Perhaps they were distant cousins?

Hudson Wells was born in Ohio as was Alvy Boles. Alvy Boles was farming in Butteville aka Butte [now Edgewood] around 1854. Before Alvy Boles went on to Fall River Mills area, for a short while, he had the first lumber mill on Boles Creek in Butteville. And after that Alvy was through there all the time.

Also the Sullaway stage coach drivers lived in Butteville. And in 1870 Johnny Hibbs lived with the Hudson Wells family in Butteville. Hibbs also had later, at one time, a dairy farm on Dairy Creek south of the town of McCloud. And there Indian Nancy, who had rescued and tended for Joaquin Miller after the Battle of Castle Crags, lived with Hibbs.

Harry L. Wells claimed no family connection to Hudson Wells, although they may have been from the same line. Wells reported in his book (Wells 1881, 134) that Hudson Wells had a milk ranch close to where John Hibbs lived on Dairy Creek in Squaw Valley. Wells told of an 1853 expedition of white men, including Dave Helm (Old Tex) who wiped out a village of Pit River Indians, who had in their possession horses stolen earlier from a Siskiyou Co. rancher.

But the 1880 census reports Hudson Wells as still living in Big Shasta Valley which is Northwest of Mt. Shasta and Dairy Creek is South of Mt. Shasta.

Also later in 1881 Frank and Chappell reported this same John Hibbs as owning the Slate Creek [now Lamoine] Hotel four miles north of Dog Creek. The stage company had a fine barn at this hotel on the Sacramento River and a Mr. Curtis was in charge of the place. Mr. George Sears ran a neat little store and saloon there. (*History and Business Directory of Shasta Co. 1881* p.31).

Chapter 3

Their Idaho Days

Alvy Boles wasn't the only story-teller Joaquin Miller met in his life time. The accompanying picture taken in Rocky Bar, Idaho in 1864 identifies for us Alvy Boles at age 53, and at age 66, the famous "Portuguese Frank" from Mendocino Co. Who was also telling stories to San Francisco journalist Ambrose Bierce. And we know that Joaquin Miller was corresponding with Ambrose Bierce as early as 1866.

In the 1860's Miller and his brother, John D., were mining in Idaho. And Joaquin, then still know as C.H.Miller, was riding pony express and, as always, writing for various papers under pseudonyms; "Old Squib," "Your Log Cabin Friend," "Esmeralda" etc. As usual, Miller was writing often about criminals from his earlier days in Shasta and Siskiyou counties. His friends were often also mentioned. Like, the *Boise News* reported "that Mr. Bledsoe on his last trip from Walla Walla, brought and presented us with an apple weighing but a small fraction less than a pound and a half." (*Boise News* Vol. 1 (52) Sept 17, 1864.

Ambrose Bierce Courtesy Bancroft Library

Not only had Joaquin Miller known Bledsoe in his own Walla Walla days, but he had known the owner/editors of the *Boise News* J.T. and T.S. Butler. They had published the *Red Bluff Beacon* in Tehama Co., California when Miller had been roping a steer for an Indian feast on Major Reading's ranch just north of Red Bluff. And Miller never met an editor he didn't cultivate forever.

For example, Frank Kenyon was owner and editor of Lewiston's *Golden* Age in those same early 1860's Idaho gold rush days. ("Cochran, Daniels and The Golden Age" Idaho State Historical Society Reference Series No. 373. July 13, 1966) Miller had known Frank Kenyon since their days of 1859 when Miller lived on Brock Creek on the Pit River. This was not far from the [Frank] Kenyon House on the stage road near the junction of Oak Run, and Reid's Toll Road at Cedar Creek (Round Mountain).

And it was from this Pitt River area and over Bullskin Ridge, Miller rode out of the mountains and down on his ill-fated trip to Millville and his alleged "horse stealing" in Churntown in 1859.

One wonders how many of the 230 names of Siskiyou Co. miners, published in the Nov. 21st 1863 *Boise News* were provided by Joaquin Miller. And it was while chasing articles signed "Esmeralda" that I found on Sept 6, 1864 that Miller had written as "Esmeralda" from Rocky Bar, Alturas Co., Idaho for the *Boise News* (Vol.2.p.4, Oct. 15, 1864):

> Ed.News: "Last night was a time long to be remembered by the citizens of this place. About sundown the people were aroused by the reverberations from the anvils of our enterprising blacksmiths Boles & Annibal. Upon inquiring the cause 'twas ascertained that three heavily laden wagons were coming in over the new wagon road just completed by that enterprising individual, Mr. Julius Newberg.

> Long and loud huzzahs rent the air and made the welkin ring. All business was for the time suspended and everybody seemed loud in their praises of the energetic and thorough-going Newberg. In commemoration of the event, at the hour of ten o'clock, about one hundred of the sturdy pioneers and business men of Rocky Bar, assembled at the Alturas Restaurant to partake of a sumptuous supper prepared on a few hours' notice by mine host Mr. Francis de Silvia, alias "Portuguese Frank." [Miller lists guest speakers and then concludes] … "after which the crowd dispersed, each wending his way to his respectable (?) place of abode as best he could." (*Boise News*, Oct. 15, 1864, p. 2 col. 4).

Rocky Bar Idaho,

L to R) Portuguese Frank, and 2 blacksmiths from Yreka Ca. Annibel and Alvy
Boles (53 years old). Oct 1864 Courtesy of Idaho State Historical Society

Rocky Bar, Idaho. Alturas Hotel

(L to R) Portuguese Frank (in apron) immediate rt Joaquin Miller, then
Nat Smith at Alturas Hotel. Courtesy Idaho State Historical Society.

This host, "Portuguese Frank" was one of Mendocino Co.'s earliest settlers and most loquacious story tellers.

Searching the Idaho State archives with the help of the The Idaho State Historical Society yielded these great pictures. First on the left is the famous "Portuguese Frank," and next was A.G. Annibal and Alvy Boles, two blacksmiths from Miller's earliest days in Siskiyou Co., CA. In the hotel picture "Portuguese Frank" was probably the man in the white apron. Historians can probably identify even more people, for it seems many were from the Shasta/Siskiyou and Mendocino Co.'s mines and ranches.

What a Yreka reunion dinner that must have been! For, Miller had met many of those men during his early days in Yreka, 1854-1859. But he only named Annibal and Boles in his 1864 Idaho news clip, because possibly they were his first Yreka friends back in 1854? Miller only wrote about Alvy Boles after his death and never wrote about Annibal.

But only a few months after these pictures ere taken the *Yreka Weekly Union* Jan. 21, 1865 reported:

> Committed Suicide. –The *Idaho Statesman* of December 16[th.] says A.G. Annibal committed suicide last week, at Rocky Bar, by taking poison. He had recently been appointed Probate Judge of Alturas Co., to fill the vacancy occasioned by the resignation of Judge Law. Deceased was a blacksmith, recently from California. It is supposed that he took this method [to] settle an account for money that he had lost in gaming. Annibal was formerly a resident of this county.

It has taken 147 years, nearly one and a half centuries, for Yreka to give Annibal his place in Siskiyou County history. The *2012 Siskiyou Pioneer p.11-32)* quotes from the "James S. Cowden

Journal" how Annibal was referred to as the leader of the wagon train leaving from Keosauqua, Iowa on the 7ᵗʰ day of April 1853- arriving in Yreka on 12 Oct. 1853. He was listed as having his wife and two children Helen and George with him. And by May 24 the journal refers to the wagon train as "Annibal's Company." We can only presume he was also in the first wagon train from Yreka, CA to Rocky Bar ID.

Perhaps Alvy Boles didn't go to Rocky Bar until 1862 or 1863. And in 1890 Bancroft's historians told us that … "on the 1ˢᵗ of May [1864] a train of eighteen wagons left Scott Valley and Yreka for Boise and on the 11ᵗʰ of June six others belonging to William Davidson taking the Yreka and Klamath Lake route ….One party of twenty three, that left Red Bluff April 24, took the route first contemplated by the California Road Company down the Malheur to the mouth of the Boise, and became lost between the Warner Lakes and the headwaters of the Malheur. They wandered about for three weeks, but finally reached their destination the 20ᵗʰ of June." (Bancroft Works, Vol. 31 *History of Washngton, Idaho, and Montana,* 1845-1889,Huberrt H. Bancroft, 1890. The History Company, Publisher San Francisco.)

Mendocino Co.'s "Portuguese Frank" could have been one of the April 19ᵗʰ 1864 party of six with pack animals from Healdsburg in adjoining Sonoma Co. which could have joined with the April 24ᵗʰ party departing Red Bluff. In any event, he and Miller's Yreka blacksmith friends, Alvy Boles and A.G. Annibal, are in the accompanying Rocky Bar Blacksmith Shop photo.

And in the Alturas Hotel photo we can identify "Portuguese Frank" by his white apron and distinctive hat, as well as by Miller's news comment about his being his "genial host". And could that be Miller by "Portuguese Frank" with one leg akimbo as shown in Joaquin's later day stage photos? We will learn more about "Portuguese Frank" later from others, but not from Miller.

Unfortunately, Harry L. Wells's 1881 *Siskiyou Co. History* didn't mention any Markhams in Siskiyou Co. so we know he hadn't seen or known of the "Partial List of Siskiyou Countians now in Boise Basin" *Boise News* Bannock City, Idaho Territory, Vol. 1:9:3:1, Nov. 21, 1863. David Markham was listed, and Miller knew him, as well as his brother Daniel Boone Markham b. in Sandusky Co. OH 12 Aug. 1822. They lived and farmed in Kansas for two years and then went to Idaho for nearly seventeen years before joining his father in Oregon in 1850. So it is no wonder that Daniel Boone Markham would have been back in Idaho during it's gold rush days and that he would have voted by proxy at a Red Bluff, CA meeting of the corporates of the "Idaho, Oregon and California Wagon Road" chaired by none other than P.B. (Pierson Barton) Reading as reported in the *Boise News* Vol. 1(33): 1:5 Sat, May 4 1864.

Miller did not tell us in the Rocky Bar newsclip in 1864 Idaho, that he personally knew, and was probably staying with David Markham on whose profitable mineral assay Miller was then reporting. And the census tells us this was the same David Markham who was born in New York, a son of Samuel Markham, whose wife ran a store in Oregon City in 1852. The Miller's tarried there in Oregon City awhile in 1852, before going on to their land claim in Lane Co. OR. This same David Markham in 1860 had a farm in Winchester, Douglas Co. OR. One could say near Roseburg, just down the road from Eugene, near where the Millers lived in adjoining Lane Co. OR. And years later Joaquin Miller is said to have been still in correspondence with this David Markham, a very much older brother to Miller's friend Edwin Markham, the poet.

Coincidentally, one finds in the 1860 census in Winchester, Douglas Co. OR, Governor Lane's son Joseph, then age 33, with a wife Elen and three children. So the Miller, Lane, and the Markham families had to have been known to each other.

Remember, the owner of the *Boise News* in Idaho had come on from Red Bluff and the young Cincinnatus Hiner Miller, by various pseudonyms, was a frequent correspondent-reporter for that paper. And P.B. Reading had known Alvy Boles since 1850. Reading was a character witness in 1859 for Joaquin Miller, when he was still the young Cincinnatus Hiner Miller, who had mined near Reading's ranch and roped a steer in early 1859 for feeding Indians on said ranch.

And it was P. B. Reading who, while trapping beaver and otter for Sutter in May of 1845, crossed the Sacramento River at Backbone. Twenty or so miles further on he discovered a river he named Trinity as he thought from Spanish maps it probably led west to "Trinity Bay." (*A History of Northern California: A Memorial and Biographical History*) Chicago, H.L. Lewis Doubleday Publishing Co., 1891, p.243).

Joaquin Miller didn't write about those closest to him and his brother John D. in their Siskiyou and Idaho mining days, until after his brother died and the others were way along in years.

For example, Miller had to have known, in Yreka, Maj. Charles McDermitt, who, with Alvy Boles had been chosen to lay out the Indian Reservation in Scott Valley right after the white miner's arrival in the 1850's. Soon after the accompanying Rocky Bar photos were taken McDermitt was killed by the Idaho Indians. And I have found no mention of this by Miller.

By 1867 a directory showed Alvy Boles as living in Yreka, his son E. A. Boles in Scott Valley and in Butte (Butteville –now Edgewood) listed the stage coach drivers Joseph and William Sulloway as well as the land developer Justin Hinckley Sisson. In those days people knew their neighbors and their comings and goings.

Wells evidently chose to totally ignore Vance Lusk Davidson and his family, also in Scott Valley by 1867, and probably related to Jeremiah and William Davidson also in Scott Valley. And, who, like the Millers, had been in Indiana before migrating to Oregon where they had lived near the Miller and Cogswell families. And Wells totally missed Joaquin Miller's Davidson and Cogswell connections. Miller's younger brother George married Lischen Cogswell who was first enamored with Joaquin's poetry and who later became one of his publishers. Brother George Miller became a real estate developer, and promoter of a highway from New York to Florence, Oregon, and designer of a "flying machine" in 1892.

And in later years Miller wrote of one of the younger Oregon Davidsons showing him through the Oregon Caves. But Miller didn't write about Scott Valley's William Davidson, although he knew him as he had known other Davidson's in Lane Co. OR and in Siskiyou Co. CA. But the census tells us that William Davidson who headed the wagon train from Yreka, CA to Rocky Bar had earlier named his son James McDermitt Davidson after his boarder, friend, and a teacher in Scott Valley - James McDermitt.

But historians and Miller have written that Miller's father, Hulings, had taught Oregon's Governor Joe Lane in school years before they all came west. But Miller didn't elaborate on other Lane Co. connections. For example, another Joe Lane married a Rebecca Davidson in Lane Co. OR June 28, 1854 the very summer that Joaquin had left Lane Co. for the California gold fields.

And Sarah J. Lemon Harden Cummins in her beautifully written 1914 auto-biography included the Davidson families in her list of emigrants to Oregon in her train in 1845. And she told how some of these then Oregonians went to California in the fall of 1848 to pan for gold, and how her father returned home in 1849 with a "coffee pot "full of nuggets worth 1900 dollars. Others stayed on or returned with their families. (Sarah J. Cummins. *Autobiography and Reminiscences,* La Grande, Oregon (1914?) Chap. VIII).

Even Wells in his book (Wells 1881, 104B) tells us that Jeremiah Davidson, before getting his land claim in Oregon, worked in a "warehouse" in Oregon City, OR in 1851. Where Mrs. Markham was running a store at the time the Hulings and Millers came along.

Joaquin Miller wrote that he first joined up in 1854 California with Oregon miners known to his father. Among these was William Davidson, perhaps as important in Scott Valley as his brother and fellow Mason, Jeremiah Davidson. And without the gift to me of Harry L.Wells' *History of Siskiyou County, California 1881* by Jeremiah's Great grandson Jim Simas in Redding CA in the 1980's I wouldn't have been able to fathom Joaquin Miller.

Jim remembered his Jeremiah Davidson grandmother sitting on the porch steps and telling to him and his 10 brothers and sisters stories about Joaquin Miller and Black Bart.

William Davidson must have been off to the mines in Idaho as early as 1860 as his wife Orpha was then listed as head of their Scott Valley household which included among many others, Charles McDermitt, age 40 and his son Charles McDermitt age 9/12. Mrs. Charles McDermitt was a sister to William Davidson

As for William Davidson, in 1864 he returned from Rocky Bar, Idaho to Scott Valley and eventually as a widower moved on to Fall River Mills. Alvy Boles then also lived nearby from 1870 onward. And it probably was at William Davidson's Scott Valley ranch that Alvy Boles' son E. A. Boles had been living and registered to vote in 1864. William Davidson was a Mason and later E. A. Boles would also be a Mason in Placerville, CA.

Since it snows heavily in Idaho and there would be no mining until spring. Perhaps William Davidson and Alvy Boles had already returned to the Davidson ranch in Scott Valley, Siskiyou Co. to spend Christmas with family. There they would have read Jan. 21 1865 that young A.G. Annibal, age 48, committed suicide back in Rocky Bar, Idaho (Nov. 28, or Dec. 1 1864 accounts differ.)

Joaquin Miller had been a sometimes contributor and a faithful reader of the *Alta California* since his arrival in 1854.

While living in Canyon City OR. Miller was a practicing attorney as well as writing for many papers including the Boise news, which he wrote under the pseudonym "Esmeralda" (the aforementioned article) about the arrival of new mining equipment. Some of his contributions included articles about David Markham in Boise.

As for "Portuguese Frank," when, why, and how, he returned to Mendocino Co., we do not know. And U.S, Census data and a raft of conflicting Mendocino legends only confuse us further. But his tombstone tells us he died Oct. 31, 1904 and that he was born Feb, 14, 1798 as Francisco Faria, in Pico, Azores while the *Mendocino Beacon* reported in 1948 that he was born same place and time but died in 1799. So we may assume he was about 66 years of age when he was photographed at the Blacksmith Shop and at the Alturas Hotel in Rocky Bar, Idaho in 1864.

Supposedly Frank went to sea at age 23 in 1821 and after several trips around Cape Horn and once around the Cape of Good Hope he landed in San Francisco and worked in some mines near Stockton, CA or operated a ferry boat out of Albion on the bay. Take your pick. Then he evidently went to Cuffey's Cove on the Mendocino Coast around 1853. then moved on in 1857 to the Big River area where Alvy's other friends C.H. English and Pierce Asbill were also located. But we do know that "Portuguese Frank" later had a bar at Comptche when he returned to Mendocino Co. and he became a great source of stories for San Francisco journalists.

Actually, Francisco Faria's nephew Louis Gonsalves came from the Azores in 1864 and together they homesteaded what is now known as the Rancho Laguna on the Comptche Ukiah Rd. (*Mendocino Country Living* Oct. 2008 p.16). And in the 1870 census Francisco Faria b. 1799 became Frank Farnier b. 1799 listed just before Louis Gonsalves in Big River Township while the Asbills were at Round Mt.in Round Valley Township but got their mail at Covelo.

Mendocino legends have it that in 1870 "Portuguese Frank" as Francisco Faria was living near his black friend Nathaniel Smith who was listed as living at Big River, in Big River Township in Mendocino Co., CA. And Mendocino legends have him on the Big River ca. 1857 when William P. and C.H Engish, and Pierce Asbill were also there. And in 1900 "Portuguese Frank" was still in Big River Township.

Mendocino area historian Rick Miller tells us that… "In 1849 Nate Smith was Captain Fletcher's cabin boy. In the early 1860's Fletcher opened up an Inn on the Navarro river. Smith left the San Francisco area for Big River (Mendocino) and settled in with the Pomo (Indians). Smith met Portuguese Frank in Mendocino. Later on both of them traveled south from the Big River to a settlement known as Elk (Cuffey's Cove is nearby). Nate and Frank were the first "white" settlers in the area. (Nate was considered white because of his light skin)."

Undoubtedly, "Portuguese Frank" could have told us better than young Frank Asbill's story in *The Last of the West* p.47-52 (1976) of how and when his father, Pierce Asbill had met up with Alvy Boles in earlier days. We can only conjecture.

Chapter 4

The Asbills

A "Biography of Pierce Asbill" does tell us in a *History of Mendocino Co.1880* that from the end of 1854-1856 Pierce and Frank Asbill were in Trinity Co. mining. And that Pierce at the end of 1856, returned to Bodega, by way of Sacramento. Pierce supposedly spent a week with his parents and then moved on to Ukiah for a season, the same time as "Portuguese Frank". Then Pierce Asbill went on to Potter Valley until the fall of 1858. He then returned to Shasta Co. until the spring of 1860. At which time he and his brothers and others went into Humboldt Co. where they had an extensive ranch until the fall of 1862.

The Asbill brothers, Pierce and Frank engaged in hunting for two years. Then they located a ranch in Summit Valley, Mendocino Co. (*History of Mendocino County, California,* Alley, Bowen & Co. Publishers, San Francisco California 1880.)

Young Frank Asbill was writing about things that happened before he was born (c.1880), and when he was a very young child. For example he writes about Black Bart being at a San Francisco hotel bar with Pierce in 1884/1885 (p.147) when Bart was actually in San Quentin. And even more unfortunately Frank Asbill never mentioned "Portuguese Frank" and we know from the pictures that he was in Rocky Bar, Idaho in 1864 while the Asbills were reportedly in Humboldt Co. But for many other years the Asbills and "Portuguese Frank" were Mendocino neighbors. But neither Pierce Asbill from his Shasta Co, days, nor "Portuguese Frank " from his Rocky Bar, Idaho days, ever mentioned that they had ever met Alvy Boles or were acquainted with Black Bart.

Another undated story is that "Portuguese Frank was in Ukiah for two years but afterwards had a bar at Melburne and lastly in Competche, Mendocino Co. All of the above mentioned locations in Mendocino Co. are within Alvy Boles' style walking distances from Black Bart's Lake (todays Clear Lake).

Napa, and Sonoma Co.'s Robberies began with No. 4. Aug. 3, 1877, and ended with No. 27 April 1883, just four miles south of Fort Ross.

Unfortunately young Frank Asbill, born in 1883, son of Pierce and nephew of Frank Asbill didn't know or had not heard of any Asbill/ "Portuguese Frank" connections, but he did know Asbill family history and their connection to the famous Black Bart.

The Asbill brothers' story was not unlike that of many other California gold miners. Their parents had both been born in Kentucky and they had been born in Missouri between1833-1836. But it differed in that Pierce, according Bancroft, had first gone to Oregon ca. 1844, thinking he had secured land but was bilked and when he brought the family out found they had no land. But they stayed awhile, learned to cure hides etc.,

Actually Pierce may have been with other Asbills when he went to Oregon in 1844. He could have been in the wagon train of Rev. E.E. Parrish who married in his wagon train May 21, 1844 an Elizabeth Asbill to a Martin Gilliam just five days before the train "camped on the Nimehaw River near the head of the Wolf and the Nimehaw in the Kickapoo country." (*Diary of Rev. Edward Evans Parrish Crossing the Plains in 1844*) 1988 p 8, 9.

Joaquin Miller evidently also knew this same Parrish family in Oregon because when Miller arrived in California he wrote to Rev. Parrish's son - also named Ed -, and wrote of Ed's sister "Merinda" as being Miller's first love. Then too, later, there was some other Parrish's living near Brock's and Miller's place on the Pit River in CA.

And of course in 1881 Harry L. Wells, knew nothing of all these connections, when he wrote:

> At all events the return of Tyee John and his fugitive companion to camp was the signal for a general massacre. That night July 23rd 1855 they [the Indians] passed down the Klamath killing all but three of the men on the river between Little Humbug and Horse Creeks. Eleven men met their death in the darkness and silence of the night. To the vigilance of a savage dog the men who escaped owed their lives. The victims were William Hennesey, Edward Parrish, Austin W. Gay, Peter Highlight, John Pollock, four Frenchmen and two Mexicans(Wells 1881, 138)

And like others in this saga, the Asbills-like the Parrish's probably became acquainted in the late 1840's with Mrs. Markham at the store in Oregon City, OR. But California's gold called and the Asbills spent a winter in Lovelock, NV waiting for the snow to clear. They were mining in 1850 in Louisville, El Dorado Co., CA. Pierce was then 19 and his brother Frank (Francis M.) 18. But in 1860 Pierce was listed with his parents at Sutter, Sacramento, CA and Frank was listed as "Asbell" with brothers R. and William in Red Bluff, CA. And some historians have Pierce mining in the Siskiyou's in the 1860's

We will have to leave it to other historians to determine when and where the Asbills first met Alvy Boles. Perhaps in those first gold rush days in the Sierras in 1850. Or was it later in 1861 when while celebrating their wealth they returned to Placerville? This according to the story as young Frank remembered hearing it from Pierce.

These Missouri Asbills were betting men and while on this celebratory trip they had made money on a foot racer while in Placerville, and had met a "bullet headed" person [Alvy Boles? –see the pictures] who had told them of how the miners in Humbug liked to bet. Alvy Boles had a mine on nearby Horse Creek.

Young Frank Asbill's story had the Asbill brothers and their foot racer being led north along lower foothill trails by the "bullet headed stranger." and supposedly crossing the Sacramento River at Kingsley's Trading Post near Red Bluff. Where actually the Asbill brothers had been trading hides for money and for Indian women.

Obviously the Asbill brothers, like everyone else, never identified Black Bart by his real name, Alvy Boles, even after Alvy died in 1890.

And surely, Joaquin Miller probably would not have known in the 1870's about any Asbill/Boles/Black Bart connection. And Miller didn't write anything about Black Bart until Bart was captured, and nothing more about Alvy Boles, as Alvy, until two years after Alvy died. In 1892 Miller told how Boles had given Miller and a young friend their first "pointer," (directions to where they should mine). Perhaps that place was near the Boles gold mine some 3.2 miles up Horse Creek from Humbug on the Klamath River.

Chapter 5

The Miller/Boles Connection

Miller did not tell, but surely he had heard, as early as his arrival in Yreka in 1854, of how in May of 1850, when Alvy Boles had first arrived in Shasta County. Alvy Boles, as Bowles, had been accused of murdering his partner on Clear Creek at what became Horsetown in Shasta Co. There was a trial with jury, and the verdict was "not guilty" because Boles's partner had been murdered by one of Ben Wright's, treacherous Oregon Indians who were camped nearby (Frank and Chappell 1881 p.21). But in 1854 Miller may have only known Alvy Boles as the man who ran pack trains between Yreka and Major Reading's ranch. Miller may not have known that in 1851 there had been a great Fourth of July Celebration in Shasta [now Old Shasta] where Major Reading had spoken, as well as then Judge W. R. Harrison, who had been Bowles defense attorney when he was found "not guilty" just the year before.

It was undoubtedly on Alvy's 1851 return from that Old Shasta celebration with his pack train to Yreka, that he took on three other men and they all became part of the famous "Seven Mules" story. Boles undoubtedly told the story to Miller in the late 1850's and then to Harry L. Wells in the 1870's. This story's location is amazingly close to where Black Bart committed his Robbery No. 13, Sept. 1, 1880. And also possibly near the never found location of the "Lost Cabin Mine" story which Wells first published on pages 116/17 of his book *History of Siskiyou County, California 1881.*

So Wells, probably between Black Bart's Sept. 16, and Sept. 22nd 1889 robberies in Oregon, or just before Bart's Siskiyou Co. robbery on Nov. 20 1880. Wells had obviously been chatting with Alvy Boles in plain sight, in Yreka. For Wells related the following Boles's story in the *Yreka Journal* Nov 27, 1880:

> 1851 spring: Alvy Boles [was] in Shasta City [now Old Shasta] buying supplies to pack on his "Seven Mules" beside which he walked to Yreka via Tower House. Three miners on good horses joined him [in Shasta] and he made them pack their horses with supplies [and walk as Alvy did] as everything expensive in Yreka. One evening camped but one day's journey from their destination" two men left camp to hunt deer and were captured by miners. Third man and Alvy proceeded to Yreka with the seven mules and three horses. Sold their goods at a considerable profit and sent to the two disappeared miners' families their share of the sold goods In August the disappeared miners showed up with great quantities of gold they had mined with the men who had captured them so as to not disclose their own find. In October, seven men and seven mules laden with cans of gold dust left for Sacramento. (Harry L. Wells *Yreka Journal* Nov. 27, 1880) [Obviously there was another miner with the two who captured the two that had been with Boles.]

But by late 1854 the pack trains from Reading's Ranch to Yreka were possibly no longer all going through Shasta and Scott Valley to Yreka but by Joe De Blondey's hostelry in the old Hastings barracks on the Sacramento River just south of Sam Lockhart's place at what we now call Dunsmuir. Gold was found on nearby Hazel Creek that summer and the Battle of Castle Crags was first reported Aug. 11 in the papers. According to the Indians, Miller was shot through the septal cartilage and recovered at Portuguese Flat only roughly 3 miles from Dog Town first settled by one of the Lytle family whom Miller had known in Oregon.

From there, on today's Dog Creek, Miller then moved South in September to Shasta City and mined, and wrote from various Sacramento River locations such as Squaw Town on Squaw Flat near Middletown, and Texas Springs, all near Major Reading's ranch.

When not mining, Miller seemed everywhere. In Shasta City he had witnessed the hanging there of Alex E. Higgins Nov. 10, 1855. Miller was making life-long acquaintances and connections everywhere, from Dr. Taliafero in Red Bluff to Father Rainaldi who opened a school in Shasta City the following year.

Between some mining and scribbling poetry in his diary Miller went to Horsetown Dec. 21 to see about enlisting with William Walker in Nicaragua but didn't think much of the terms being offered.

So he returned to mining and Jan. 1856 found Miller participating in a miners meeting about tearing out dams of the Texas Springs Ditch so as to provide water for the Tadpole miners.

In April he wrote a spoof about Squaw Town being the city of the future and in May he bought a horse which he pastured at the American Ranch now known as Anderson. That month, the miners of Jackass Flat went on strike for cheaper water. But Miller had evidently made enough to retrieve his new mare and soon headed back to his Indian friends up on the McCloud River. He "bid adieu" to Squaw Town July 7, 1856 loaded down with arms and ammunition which others might have carried on up the Pit River. Miller arrived back at Portuguese Flat July 11, for only four days. Then went on to Lower Soda Springs further up the Sacramento River and thence returned to Squaw Valley that summer.

Some accounts tell of him building a cabin near Heckathorn's place in Squaw Valley south of the present town of McCloud. Miller's first cabin building experience had been in helping his father and his eldest brother cut logs and make a cabin at Sunny Ridge, Oregon. He then would have then been only about 14 years old.

And now only three years later in California Miller was supposedly building his first cabin not far from where an Indian village had been wiped out in the spring of 1853 by a group of men from Dunsmuir in retaliation for Indian horse stealing. An estimated 200 head of horses had been stolen in 1851 from Shasta Valley and surrounding areas. ("Excerpts from the Siskiyou County Comprehensive Land & Resource Management Plan February 1996" *Klamath Bucket Brigade).* Note some modern writers suggest that Miller taught the Indians how to steal horses. He hadn't even left Indiana, as a child, in 1851.

A letter written by Miller was posted from Lower Soda Springs Nov. 26 1856 but he writes elsewhere that it was on these same trails that he had in December re-crossed Squaw Mountain near Girard Ridge to winter at Soda Springs. Probably to spend the holidays with the Ross McCloud family on land on the Sacramento River they had bought from Lockhart at Upper Soda Springs where old Bill *Tauhindali (*Towendolly), -Frank La Pena's ancestor, had stayed on as caretaker. But elsewhere in his writing Miller indicates he was living with the Indians at *Ah-Di-Na* on the McCloud River when the massacre occurred over at Fall River in the winter of 1856/57. This is an excellent example of Wells's correct criticism of Miller for having made Siskiyou history into his own personal history.

But it was Harry L. Wells who sometimes also missed real history. For in his book *History of Siskiyou County, California 1881*, historian Wells reported that an A (Adam this time) Boles was killed by Indians during the massacre when all the time Wells was interviewing Alvy Boles in Yreka and Shasta Valley for his 1881 history.

Chapter 6

After the Massacre

==============

Right after the massacre had been reported in the 1857 newspapers, young Miller, who had been living with the *Wintu* Indians on the McCloud River, judiciously joined the white avengers from Yreka. Only to flee from their ranks after their retaliatory raid against the Pit River Indians and return to live with his Indian friends on the McCloud River. Oh yes, plus a short winter stint at college back in Eugene, Oregon from November 1857 until February 1858.

Perhaps in the Spring Miller returned to mining in the Clear Creek area, as a few months later into 1858 we find Miller was roping a steer on Major Reading's ranch for the purpose of feeding Reading's Indians. Shortly thereafter Miller was engaged in buying guns and ammunition in Old Shasta for other Indians, possibly Pit Rivers, to use in yet another uprising against the whites.

Today everyone knows of Miller's flight from Old Shasta in 1859, his borrowing or stealing of a horse in Churntown, his escape up the Sacramento River and Lower Salt Creek to *Matquaw* Flat. There he was apprehended by fellow miners, the same place where my husband fished his last time just before he died.

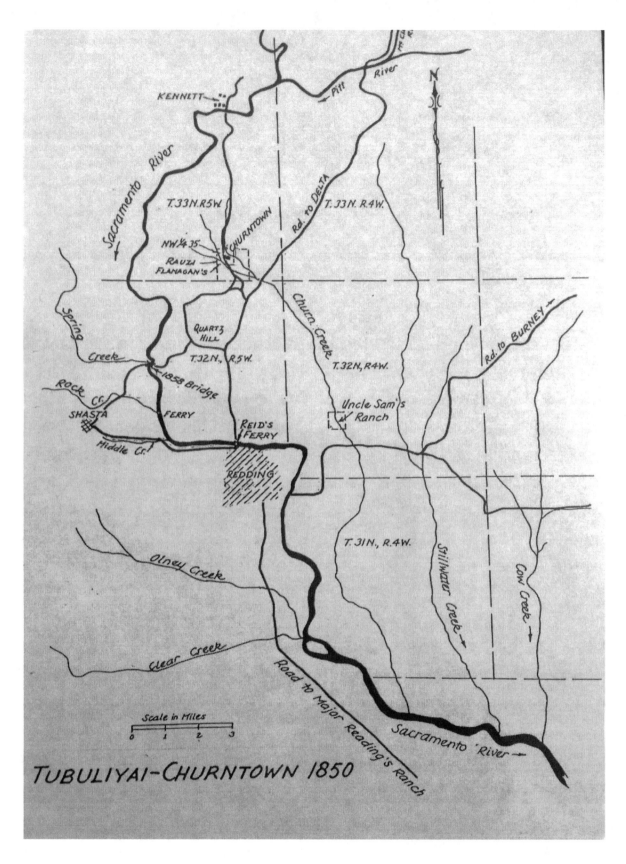

Tubuliyai-Churntown 1850

We had first visited that old Indian site while my Dad, Frank I. Guilford, was involved with developing it for Oakland Boys club. My husband John R. Kardell had built for them a dam to make a swimming pool in Lower Salt Creek.

Back in 1859 Miller was indicted and jailed in Old Shasta but (supposedly?) escaped on the Fourth of July. Later Major Reading testified on his behalf and Anton Roman, later a bookstore owner in San Francisco, held on to Miller's poems. Archibald Skillman, editor of the *Shasta Courier*, had been, and continued to publish Miller's work, all written under pseudonyms. And the general opinion was that it would be fine if Miller just disappeared and quit stirring up revolt amongst Indians.

But Sam Lockhart, (still crazed by the death of his twin brother Harry, killed by the Indians in Fall River area), tracked Miller to Jim Brock's place on the Pit River. He then took Miller back to Yreka to be tried by Judge Rosborough for complicity in Harry Lockhart's murder by the Indians.

Few have realized that Judge Rosborough although born in South Carolina in 1817, was listed in the 1850 Census as living in El Dorado Co. CA while Alvy Boles was listed in adjoining Calaveras Co., CA. Also in El Dorado Co. in 1850 was a John L. [Lytle] Cummins and in 1855 Dr. J. Lytle Cummins and a fellow by the name of Slade bought the *Mountain Herald* in Yreka. So Miller, the young aspiring journalist who had known Lytle and Cummins families in Oregon, would have pursued a friendship with Dr. Cummins who was in the second party to ascend Mt. Shasta. And surely, just as young Miller would have visited the Davidsons he knew in Scott Valley he also would have visited Andrew J. Lytle (b. OH and also recently from Oregon) who was the first to homestead in 1855 in the Dog Creek area on the Sacramento River just downriver from where Miller was living with Joe DeBlondey. (Dottie Smith *Record Searchlight*

Blog Aug. 27, 2013) The Dog Creek area is where Alvy Boles had earlier, in 1850, led the miners from Readings Ranch North to Boles Creek, then on to Yreka. Miller probably didn't know that the Davidson and Lytle Families had connections dating back to the 1700's in Pennsylvania. But Miller surely knew that there was a Lytle Bar on or near Lytle Flat on the Scott River below Scott Bar (Wells 1881 ibid p. 192. 217)

Judge Rosborough had arrived in 1853, about the same time as Miller, and was in business with Sam Lockhart in building the Lockhart Wagon Rd. from the Noble Pass Trail to Yreka through Fall River valley. Perhaps the judge even knew from Sam's bragging, how Sam and his brother Harry supposedly had left strychnine laced flour on tree stumps for starving Indians.

It was over this Lockhart Wagon Rd. that historians tell us that Rogers and Bowles [our Alvy Boles] took their saw mill equipment, most likely from Butteville [Edgewood], over into the Fall River Valley the summer before the massacre in the 1856. And surely by 1859 Yreka's Judge Rosborough already knew from Alvy Boles how he had escaped the massacre. Since Rosborough probably often saw Alvy, or his son, E. A. Boles, then living in Yreka with the famous Rufus Johnson.

Imagine being the 18 year old E.A. Boles (b.OH) living with the 37 year old Rufus Johnson (b. MO) who led his party of miners from the coast up the Trinity River to Yreka Creek in 1850 to where Gov. Lane's Oregon group were already prospecting.

Judge Rosborough knew all of these people from his everyday life. Alvy was not dead and there was no way Miller could have been involved in the massacre. So Judge Rosborough just dismissed the charges or just let Miller go free. The records are not clear.

So why has there been so much confusion in all the writings about this Alvy Boles who befriended Miller? Because in his first days in Yreka, it was Alvy who had given Miller his first mining pointer, and Alvy certainly hadn't been killed by the Indians.

In the 1970s Redding's Judge Eaton and I discovered Alvy was alive and listed as a blacksmith in census years after 1870. So, why all the confusion and obfuscation about someone in plain sight?

Judge Eaton being the son of Edna Behrens Eaton, who would have known most newspaper men, as her brother was a journalist in San Francisco around the same time as Joaquin Miller and Ambrose Bierce. Edna also knew May Hazel Southern from the Historical Society. Judge Eaton would have grown up knowing the story of Alvy Boles, but he was letting me grow in my pursuit of the truth.

Chapter 7

Alvy Boles in Yreka

Who was this Alvy Boles? This blacksmith who was chosen on Oct. 29, 1851 along with Charles McDermitt by the leading Citizen's Committee of Shasta Butte (Yreka). They were to ride with Col. McKee's & George Gibbs party to investigate a suitable location for an Indian reservation. They rode out the following morning Oct. 30th and a part of Scott Valley was decided upon, and a treaty signed Nov. 4, 1851.

Charles McDermitt was a good choice because he had been early in the area having arrived at Joe Lane Bar where Yreka Creek empties into the Shasta River in the summer of 1850. And in 1852 McDermitt headed a company of volunteers who rode with Ben Wright to the relief of immigrants struggling though Modoc Co. en route to Yreka. McDermitt also became the first Sheriff as well as building the first large house in Yreka.

Alvy Boles also had been a good choice because he and Dr. William Dane had been among the first to arrive in Yreka (Wells, 1881, 199). They ran a pack train and were also starting to build a hospital. In the Appendix you may learn more about that "Seven Mule" pack train Alvy had brought from Shasta City through Scott Valley in just that spring of 1851.

Alvy Boles and Dr. Dane's first large building in Yreka failed as a hospital. But Alvy had also planted, surely with paid Indian help, 20 acres in vegetables, barley, oats, and wheat over in Shasta Valley at Butteville [Edgewood]. These products he sold to the miners at fair prices during the following "starving winter" when supplies did not get through and others were gouging the miners. Some of the grains he sold as seed.

Miller knew this story first hand as he had arrived in Yreka as it played out and he wrote it into his own stories about himself, the Indians, and the miners first in the local papers, then in his books.

"Pappa had never understood business and my experience in the gold fields wasn't improving my opinion either, hence his "The Trader "(*Courier* 7/23/ 59) signed "Skurb.").

> ...
> But up where the fleecy torrents fall,
> 'Mid the mountains cragg'd and old,
> When rock and river and tree and all
> Are buried deep in one silent pall,
> Ghastly, unbroken and cold—
> The trader gloats o'er his full supplies,
> While round him stalks Hunger gaunt—
> He strengthens his bolts and raises his price,
> With "Pay me double and pay me thrice,
> Pay me in gold or perish for want!" ...

Miller claimed to have never heard of a fair merchant except his old friend Alvy Boles who had raised potatoes in Shasta Valley in 1852 and sold them at a fair price--even some on credit--all during a hard winter.

Boles had given Miller and his young partner their first location tip when they first tried mining on their own in late 1854. They were grubstaked by Frank Campbell of the Humbug saloon -- and

Miller later wrote about this in his "Little Gold Miners of the Sierras" for the children's magazine *Wide Awake* (10/83).

Yes, you are on the "clewe" trail! Black Bart's last robbery was Nov. 3, 1883 and he began serving his sentence Nov. 21, 1883. Now, how long before that had Miller correctly guessed Bart's identity? and with this story in *Wide Awake* was Miller as a friend, journalist and lawyer, merely setting straight the history of Alvy Boles who had been so helpful to Miller in his early years in the mines?

Miller remembered how even though Alvy had become Yreka's first Constable and written out the first warrant for an arrest in that area. The populace rejected Alvy's later bid for Justice of Peace, saying he was "too honest" for the job because he had sold his potatoes at fair prices. Miller also remembered Alvy was carrying on commerce by pack mule train with Major Reading whose oats were needed in Yreka and the mines.

Miller possibly met Major Reading through Alvy Boles who probably had first met Major Reading when Alvy had been tried for murder, but acquitted by Judge W.R. Harrison. While mining for gold on Clear Creek in 1850's Alvy Boles [written as Bowles] was accused of murdering a co miner, later it was proved he was murdered by Oregon Indians.

But, why had I in the 1970's become so curious about Alvy Boles as well as Joaquin Miller? Was it because I lived on *Matquaw* (Spirit) Mt. overlooking the McCloud River part of Shasta Lake? Or because I had been finding that jealous academic journalists, and local historians had for years been titillating readers with slanted stories about Miller and his life with the Indians. About his stay in Shasta's jail, and his association with miscreants and robbers like Black Bart?

Much of what was written I had found proven to be not true. Also, I found in my research "What Bart Says," (a piece obviously written by Joaquin Miller, using the name "Martin"). Published in 1888 after Bart was released from jail. "Martin's" story traveled Miller over trails through *Matquaw* Flat on down to the McCloud River and over the mountains. On across Squa Valley Creek, then down to a place where Miller earlier lived at Jim Brock's place on Brock Creek which emptied into the Pit River. This same place where Alvy Boles could have fled to when he escaped the Fall River Indian Massacre in the winter of 1856.

In 1922 J.P. Harrington identified Brock's place as *lolosquton* (shallow water bar old place) on the Pit River at the mouth of Brock Creek. In *Wintu, ton* usually referred to a place where there had been a village a very long time ago. And it was just short of a mile upriver from *Norelputis*'s last village on the Pit River occupied by the *Wintu* in the 1850's. This village is identified in the 1980's as # 126 *Hlolok* (beard of grass or grain) a village with about ten houses and a headman named *Pantiqilili* (on top called out to somebody) (Occas. Papers #1 p. 58).

So Brock's 1850 place still had a *Wintu* name known to Harrington's *Wintu* guide in 1922. His other guides also gave him the *Yana* and Pit River names of the place on the Backbone Ridge. From there you went down a trail north to the Pit River to Brock's Place which would indicate it was, and had been, a main north/south east/west cross point for years, for the Indians of all groups, *Yuki, Yana, Wintu*, Pit River, Coastal, and perhaps Eastern tribes.

And in the early 1850's, while living at Brock's place, this famous Indian crossing, was Miller's access southwesterly to Millville, Reading's ranch, and Shasta. And it was probably Alvy Bole's refuge after the 1856 massacre, and before, and after his Fern// Whitmore robbery Oct. 27, 1879 and his two robberies – Oct. 25, 1879 and Sept. 18, 1882 at Bass Hill and all in Shasta Co.

After my first ten years of research it became obvious to me that

Alvy Boles's life and Black Bart's Robberies had all taken the same paths. Even Collins and Levene's 1992 *Black Bart* had unwittingly separated the robberies into four different locales, each of which had been where Alvy Boles had also lived or worked.

And then there were little tidbits, such as George Albro's story after seeing Bart's 1883 after-capture picture. Albro said, "I remember seeing him around the stable in Old Shasta." But Albro never knew or chose not to remember Black Bart's real name.

In the 1980's when asked to speak at a Shasta Historical Society Meeting about Joaquin Miller I postulated that Black Bart was an itinerant blacksmith who was well recognized by all as Alvy Boles.

Lola Hawes Schwartz spoke up saying her family had a wooden mantle piece made from a piece of a barn beam on which the "Black Bard" had once carved the initials "B.B." probably after shoeing their horses. The Hawes Ranch was also well known as the "Fort Ranch" as it adjoined Fort Reading where Alvy Boles had also shoed horses.

This bookkeepers recognition story was again validated in 1994 when Ursula Watkins gave to me Greg Watkins' story about a person calling himself "Martin" working seasonally in the sawmill at the Reader Ranch in Nevada Co. CA. (Greg Watkins, grandson of Frank and great grandson of Jim Reader Feb.1987-Jan.1993). ATheir bookkeeper who was later working in San Francisco's Palace Hotel in 1883 when Black Bart was captured. This is just around the corner from the Webb House where Black Bart was captured. Black Bart was held in the San Francisco City Jail until transferred to San Quentin. Of course when the bookkeeper saw the picture of Black Bart in the newspaper he recognized him as the "Mr. Martin". The bookkeeper informed the them at the Reader Ranch.

Recently, I found historian Bob Wyckoff's article about "Mr.

Martin" in *The Union Newspaper* Oct. 25, 2003 which validates and expands on Greg Watkins account. Wyckoff was the photographer who took part in the interview of Frank Reader, age 92, in Feb. 1962. Like everyone else's report; their Bart was "well dressed, had a Victorian manner and spoke well in a deep voice." Frank also remembered that "Mr. Martin" was always polite etc. as had all other accounts. But no one had a "clewe" as to who Black Bart really was.

Much of the real history of Joaquin Miller and Black Bart may never come to light. Part of that could be because of an earlier sense of editorial discretion. For example, back in 1859 when Miller was either in jail and/or fleeing from the law Skillman as editor at the *Courier* was still receiving mail from Miller. In print Skillman acknowledged some printing errors Miller had caught in some of his published poems and so he published an untitled poem, and "A Bolter"(*Shasta Courier* (Jul. 30/1859) which referred to someone changing their political party rather than to Miller's escape from jail.

Miller's parting political shot as "Skurb" was his 'Lection Time (*Courier* 9/ 3/1859) "By Skurb."):

> ...
> Lager beer and lobster lunches,
> Cobblers cool and soothing punches.
> Slings and cocktails most sublime,
> Whisky-straights if any choose 'em,
> Havanas for all who use 'em,
> Lay round loose in 'lection time! ...

By then Miller was back up north in Washington Territory teaching school for a settler in Clark Co. on the Oregon River (which came to be called the Columbia). This is near Vancouver,

Washington for the Fall session when in Oct. or Nov. of 1859 General Scott, landed at Fort Vancouver to join Harney on his way to San Juan Island. Miller took his class to see his ship. Scott was there because of the Pig War on San Juan Island when it was in dispute between the British and Americans. Miller wrote about these times in "The Continuous Woods." *The Independent* (Aug. 15/1889).

Chapter 8

From Trails to Stage Roads

But in 1859 Miller's heart was still back in his mountains with his mining friends and his Indians. He had letters about all the unrest such as that described in the *Shasta Herald* (Dec. 31/59).

"From the Indian Country: We learn, thro' an old friend, Mr. John B. Sluicer, who lives in the mountains high up on Cow Creek, that large numbers of Indians are gathering in the Big Bend of Pit River. Not less than 1500 Indians are in that section of the country. They are mostly of the tribe called *Chenewas [Achumawi* according to linguists]. A bad feeling exists among them towards the whites, and there are various rumors of plots against the settlers. It is altogether likely there will be trouble soon. It is regretted, among those living on the borders that Kibbe's Rangers have been disbanded and the expedition terminated.

These Indians are now driven by the snows into the valleys, where they could easily be captured and taken out of the country."

The Indians evidently knew where John B. Sluicer lived on upper Cow Creek and he was soon after shot by many Indian arrows and died. (Sept. *Sacramento Daily Union* Sept. 3, 1860)

Now Sluicer's place was only about ten "as the crow flies" miles east of Brock's cabin at the mouth of Brock Creek on the Pit River. Where earlier, in 1859 after Miller had escaped from jail in Shasta, Sam Lockhart had tracked him down. Sam was convinced Miller had been complicit in the January 1857 massacre where Sam's twin brother Harry had been killed at Fall River. Sam had been searching out and killing any Indians he thought were involved. Sam was well known in the area having reputedly built the first building in Yreka while at the same time owning a saloon somewhere in Shasta Valley, possibly Butteville [Edgewood].

Surely Sam Lockhart knew of the close connections between Joaquin Miller and Joe Lane in Yreka. Both men were down from Oregon and both formerly from Indiana. Perhaps Sam even knew that the Lane and Brock families had been neighbors in Indiana and previously in Virginia. So Brock's cabin on the Indian's trail from the Fall River area down to Reading's Grant on the Sacramento River was a logical place to search for Miller.

And it was obvious that Sam Lockhart, Joaquin Miller, and Alvy Boles had all been using the same trails since 1854. Back then the Sacramento River became more important and the trail went north from Lower Soda Springs on up the Sacramento River through what is now Weed. Then the trail continues on along Boles Creek to Butteville [Edgewood], and on to Yreka. 1854 was also the year that Ross McCloud bought from the twin Lockhart brothers, Sam and Harry, their 160 acres, complete with cabin and split rail fence. Which they had built on their 1852 squatters rights land, at Upper Soda Springs on the Sacramento River, just a few miles north of where Miller lived with Joe de Blondey in 1854/1855. Sam and Harry earlier had a hotel in Humbug in 1851. When young C.H. Miller had joined De Blondey, these places became competing hostelries.

Sam Lockhart was well known to the courts too. The first order on the record of the Siskiyou court bears date May 13/52, the day after the county officers were sworn in. It read as follows: James Stevenson vs. .Samuel Lockhart and others who owed James Stevenson $910.62.

It had been Sam Lockhart who finally opened a trail north from Manzanita Lake in the shadow of Mt. Lassen, as a spur of Nobles Trail, which crossed the Sierra Nevada's from Roop's Fort (now Susanville) to Yreka. The first movement in the direction of a wagon road in that area had been made in 1852 by Col. James L. Freaner, the "Mustang" newspaperman of Mexican war notoriety. With John Brando, Jackson, Warren, and a Mexican known as Adobe John. Freaner had started out to locate a wagon road, going by way of Sheep Rock and Pit River. Nothing more was heard of this party until four years later when the Indians disclosed the fact that they had murdered them on Pit River. Nothing further was done in the matter till A.M. Rosborough and Samuel Lockhart undertook to lay out a road on the same route in the spring of 1856. Lockhart went over it with an ox-team, and then piloted a Mormon train of thirty-five wagons down his trail. The Lockhart brothers established a ferry on Fall River with a toll license from Shasta .Co.

That fall the Indians also attacked a stage driven by Jerry Robbins on this trail and he managed to reach safety, but he was all full of arrows.

That was the winter of 1856/57 while Miller was presumably living with the *Wintu* on the McCloud River and in Squaw Valley.

Harry Lockhart, Rogers, Alvy Bole's and others decided to winter in Fall River Valley rather than to return to Yreka. According to historians, who were not there, all in the valley were massacred.

Not true, as Alvy Boles, who had given Miller his first mining tip, survived but that story comes later.

When reported back to Yreka in 1857 the killings brought forth the Pit River Rangers. This was citizen's militia contingent from Yreka, of which Miller had to be a part of to prove his innocence to Lockhart, and the boys in the mines. It was a short war, since Lockhart had his ferry repaired and back in service in time for freight teams to reach Yreka from Red Bluff by the middle of May.

In 1858 a man named McElroy built a toll bridge across the Pit River a short distance above Lockhart's ferry. But, he too was supposedly killed by Indians. And in the fall of 1859, McElroy's brother was shot in the back by one of his own party while leading a group of local men in an attack on an Indian village.

Sam Lockhart built another bridge of his own in the fall and Sam went on killing Indians in revenge for his Brother Harry's death.

Miller probably read in the *Shasta Courier* Sept l, 8, and 15th. That on the 8th of Aug. 1860 a J. W. Chaffee was drowned in the Pit River near Lockhart's Ferry. It was reported in Shasta by Isaac Gibson who charged Lockhart had killed Chaffee. Sheriff Follansbee, Squire Keene J.P --father of Miller's friend Jim Keene-, and District Attorney Mix, went to Pit River to disinter the body and hold an inquest with a jury of all they could find. Others later said these were all enemies and it was found that the man had been "rendered" stupid by blows from Lockhart, had fled to the river and was drowned. Witnesses at the hearing testified otherwise and Justice Keene could only make it ordinary assault. He therefore, fined Lockhart $10.00 and costs. It is proper to say that Mr. Lockhart came voluntarily to Shasta when the charge was made against him for the purpose of having a legal investigation there being no justice resident in the Pit River Valley. But Lockhart's counsel succeeded in having the case transferred to Justice Shed's Court.

Lockhart had always thought Miller was in with the Indians in the Fall River Valley massacre despite Miller's later service with the militia. And he surely knew of Miller's alleged horse borrowing incident in Shasta, and Miller's escape from the jail in Shasta, as Lockhart was also a reader and contributor of news to the *Shasta Courier.*

> For example (Apr. 30/59), "Sam Lockhart arrived in town on yesterday, in two days from Fort Crook. He informs us that the trail to the Fort is now open." Also "that the recent water backed up on some of the bottom land, and seriously injured several fields of grain." warm weather and rain raised Pit River five feet higher than it has ever been before.

Evidently Sam was in town on his own legal business because the *Shasta Courier* (May 7/59) reported: "Court of Sessions. Honorable Joel T. Landrum, Judge.
On May 3 People vs. Lockhart; withdraws plea of
'not guilty' and pleads guilty of assault; waives
usual time for sentence, and was sentenced to pay
a fine of $1 and costs of prosecution."
But Lockhart's counsel succeeded in having the case transferred to Justice Shed's Court and evidently thence transferred to Landrum. Lockhart got off lighter than Miller did. Miller was indicted by a Grand Jury in Shasta Co. and a warrant issued, but by then, as you know, Miller was freed by Judge Rosborough in Siskiyou Co., and on his way to Washington Territory.

However, Sam Lockhart wasn't through suspecting Miller of complicity and they would cross paths again over in Silver City, Idaho.

Miller and Lockhart had know each other since in Humbug and Lockhart's full story is set to come out by Will Snyder in his forth coming book tenantively titled "LOCKedHART" which further verifies of the names and places of Alvy Boles associates in Shasta and Siskiyou Counties.

Chapter 9

Gold Mining

But, back to the Miller and Black Bart saga. It was Miller's father's friend Governor Lane of Oregon Territory who was one of the first prospectors in Yreka's vicinity, in July or August, 1850. Though Rufus Johnson's party entered by way of Trinity River and prospected the eastern districts in 1850 and was on Yreka Creek also in August.

According to notes copied from Miller's diary he had left Oregon Oct. 23/54, arriving in Yreka on the 12th of Nov. /54. He spent the winter mining and cooking for miners in that vicinity, in company with some Oregonians whom he had formerly known. He made enough to "buy me a good horse, a mule and a good outfit."

In all of Miller's books, articles and poems on the men and days of '49, the real essence of the white man's mining experience is condensed in this one simple statement in his 1873 *Life Amongst the Modocs*:

> "Every man there who bent above the boulders, and toiled on silently under the dark plumed pines and the shadows of the steep and stupendous mountains, was a giant in body and soul.

Never since the days of Cortez has there been gathered together such a hardy and brave body of men as these first men of the Pacific.

When it took six months' voyaging round the Horn, and imminent perils, with like dangers and delays, to cross the Isthmus or the continent, then the weak of heart did not attempt it and the weak of body died on the way.

The result was a race of men worthy of the land. The world's great men were thus drawn out, separated and set apart to themselves out here on the Pacific. There was another aggregation and sifting out after the Pacific was reached. There lay the mines open to all who would work; no capital but a pick and pan required. The most manly and independent life on earth.

At night you had your pay in your hand, your reward weighed out in virgin gold. If you made five, ten, fifty, or a thousand dollars that day, you made it from the fall of no man; no decline of stocks or turn in trade which carried some man to the bottom and brought you to the top; no speculation, no office, no favour, only your own two hands and your strong true heart, without favour from any man. You had contributed that much to the commerce of the world. If there is any good in gold, you had done that much good to the world, beside the good to yourself. What men took this line of life!

But some preferred to trade, build towns, hang about them, and practice their wits on their fellow-men.

You see at once that the miners were the cream of the milk in this second separation."

In one of Miller's later poems he sang the story this way:

Lo! When the last pick in the mine
Is rusting red with idleness,
And rot yon cabins in the mold,
And wheels no more creak in distress,

And tall pines re-assert command,
Sweet bards along this sunset shore
Their mellow melodies will pour--
Will charm as charmers very wise--
Will strike the harp with master hand--

Will sound unto the vaulted skies
The valour of these men of old--
The mighty men of 'Forty-Nine--
Will sweetly sing and proudly say,
Long, long ago there was a day
When there were giants in the land.

What gold mining did to the land he often referenced but this one stanza says it all:

God gave us Mother Earth full blest
With robes of green in healthful fold
We tore the green robes from her breast
We've sold our mother's robes for gold.

What gold mining did to destroy the Indians was the theme of much of Miller's work. His 1873 *Life Amongst the Modocs* covered Indian genocide as effected by massacres led by early gold miners.

It was both an autobiographical and historical novel, his best accepted book. His harder hitting 1881 *Shadows of Shasta* written for dramatization covered the land grabbing and reservation round-up phase of Indian extermination, but was so close to life that it closed with unresolved tragedy. Miller's personal pain and anger even showed in an unconscious lapse into first person in one part of the story. In the Introduction he wrote:

> "It is impossible to write with composure or evenness on this subject. One wants to rise up and crush things.... We are making dreadful history, dreadfully fast. How terrible it will all read when the writer and reader of these lines are long since forgotten! Ages may roll by.
>
> We may build a city over every dead tribe's bones. We may bury the last Indian deep as the eternal gulf. But these records will remain, and will rise up in testimony against us to the last day of our race."

Shasta, Siskiyou, and Modoc Counties were not the only places where Indians were being eliminated or relocated. Mendocino Co. suffered similarly from an invasion of land seekers more than gold seekers. First came the Spanish and the Russians, then American land seekers moving on from their mining stints in the Sierras. Cattle and sheep grazing overtook the Indians and other players moved into this story of Joaquin Miller and the Real Black Bart.

Chapter 10

"More Clewes"

Our first "clewe" to Black Bart's real identity came from George Wharton James in his *Exposition Memories San Diego 1916.* The Radiant Life Press 1917, p. 62 tells us that when Edwin Markham "...was a tender of sheep in the Suisun valley," that Markham "and a companion ventured into the woods in Mendocino County ... he was solicited by a vigorous looking man to accompany him on a money making trip. This man afterward proved to be a noted bandit and highway man who served a term in San Quentin."

Edwin Markham left us a poem about his climb into the woods of Mendocino Co.:

A Mendocino Memory

I climbed the canyon to a river head,
And looking backward saw a splendor spread,
Miles beyond miles, of kingly hue
And trembling at the limbs of Arras knew-
A flowering pomp as of the dying day,
A splendor where a god might take his way.

It was the brink of night and everywhere
Tall redwoods spread their filmy tops in air;

Huge trunks, like shadows upon shadows cast,
Pillared the under twilight, vague and vast.

Lightly I break green branches for a bed,
And gathered ferns, a pillow for my head.
And what to this were kingly chambers worth-

When Markham published this poem in 1916 he was thinking back to a time when he was in Mendiciono Co. When "Portuguese Frank" would have been there also, long before going to Rocky Bar Idaho in 1863/64. (See Rocky Bar Blacksmith photo on page 23)

Was Markham at the riverhead of the Noyo River that empties into the ocean at Fort Bragg in Mendocino Co.? Fort Bragg is only about 13 miles, "as the crow flies", from Willits, and by road, today around 33 miles.

Think back to the Idaho gold rush days of the 1860's, and the picture of Alvy Boles with "Portuguese Frank", from Mendocino Co., and the accompanying article in September 1864 by Joaquin Miller, under pseudonym, *Esmeralda*, about Rocky Bar Idaho. And Miller's article under his own name, Hiner Miller, about David Markham's profitable mineral assay in Idaho at roughly the same time.

We obviously must conclude that when Alvy Boles was offering a job to young Edwin Markham on a trail in Mendocino Co., say around 1868, that they both knew who the other person was.

Our last "clewe" as to a Markham connection came in 2012 from Linda Markham Curry, Great Great grandniece of Edwin Markham. It seems Edwin had a brother John Bird Markham living in Pope Valley in adjoining Sonoma Co. John moved on to Idaho in 1880 and then to the Bay Area. John Bird Markham, b.1831 in Michigan, would have been 21 when the Millers arrived in Oregon

City, OR in 1852, and shopped in Mrs. Markham's store. Joaquin Miller's brother, John D. b. in 1837, would have been 15.

Samuel and perhaps John Bird, like many Oregonians, went to California to mine for a while. Since Samuel Markham had led a wagon train to Oregon in 1847 and had been in Ohio in first Erie, then Sandusky Co. from1810 to 1825 it is obvious that these ex Ohio residents were more than nodding acquaintances in the West.

Another early "clewe" to the fact that Black Bart had ties to people and fore-knowledge of terrain where he committed his robberies came from Collins and Levene's maps showing the clustering of Bart's robberies. For example, portions of Lake, Napa, Mendocino, and Sonoma Cos. included Robberies Nos. 4, 7. 8. 12, 22, 23, 26, and 27.

In any event, we know that Alvy Boles in 1870 could have been back to running his pack trains from Yreka through to Sonoma and Mendocino counties. And Collins and Levene's 1992 *Black Bart* (p.89) tells us about a robbery July 22, 1880 (#12), when John Orr's driver James Curtis was "stopped at Sheep House Gulch on Markham's ranch near Duncan's Mill" in Sonoma Co. Their Historical Society's 1963 *Journal* Vol. 1 tells us that the Markham place was part of the 17,600 acre Muniz [Munoz] Rancho that stretched from Timber Cove to Duncan's Mills. Possibly that was not a Markham ranch related to Samuel's family as there were innumerable unrelated Markham families in several coastal counties.

But many of the early miners in Yreka relocate later back to Mendocino Co. And Rufus Johnson who in 1850 led miners from the coast into Yreka, was living in the same house in Yreka with Alvy Boles's son, E. A. while Alvy was off in the new mines in Idaho in the 1860's.

Circumstances didn't cause Black Bart to start robbing stages until 1875, five years after encountering young Edwin Markham in the Mendocino Forest and offering him a job probably working with Alvy Boles on yet another pack train.

Bart's first robberies in Mendocino Co. were actually his # 7 and #8 on Oct. 2nd and 3rd, 1878. But there are conflicting stories about his whereabouts during that time. The October 2, Mendocino Co. robbery occurred only twelve miles from Ukiah; and Bart was reported as having been seen picnicking (eating apples) along the roadside before the robbery.

According to one account, after the October 3, 1878 robbery of the stage from Covelo to Ukiah. Bart walks to the McCreary farm and pays for dinner. "Fourteen-year-old Donna McCreary provides the first detailed description of Bart: Graying brown hair, missing two of his front teeth, deep-set piercing blue eyes under heavy eyebrows, slender hands and intellectual in conversation, well flavored with polite jokes."

Also, George Hoeper wrote in 1995 that in the fall of 1880 Mrs. McCreary of Potter Valley remembered that earlier that year in June she had served lunch to the man then known as Black Bart. (*Black Bart Boulevardier Bandit*, p.51).

Actually, Frank Asbill's Mendocino recollections in his *Last of the West* 1975, seems more accurate. Although they had to have come from hearsay stories from his father, Pierce Asbill, as Frank wasn't born until 1883 the year Black Bart was apprehended and landed in San Quentin. Where Frank also landed many years later.

And evidently unknown to Frank was the Asbill/Portuguese Frank/ Alvy Boles connection from 1864 onward. Also Frank Asbill never heard of Alvy Boles because Pierce Asbill, the Markhams, Joaquin Miller, and everyone else always referred to Black Bart as C.E. Boles or Charles Bolton (in Joaquin Miller's 1888 "What

Bart Says" Miller said "...having known Bolton when he was a mining man..." That is the name to which Black Bart agreed to when he was arrested. No one who really ever knew Alvy Boles ever identified him by name, as being Black Bart. Not Miller, not Markham, not Davidson, not Southern, or even an old George Albro who, as a boy, had worked in Shasta's stable.

Frank Asbill's *Last of the West* was all about a person called "a stranger" whom his father, Pierce, and his Uncle Frank had met in Placerville in 1864. They had gone there with a pack train of gold to celebrate their success in life. Frank repeated stories he heard from them about their celebrating in the saloons and betting on a foot racer who won. They also met a "bullet headed stranger" who offered to lead them and the foot racer to a mining town (Humbug in Siskiyou Co.) where miners would bet on anything, and the Missouri Asbills could win big.

This "stranger" the Asbills met in Placerville in 1864 was undoubtedly Alvy Boles on his way back from the Idaho mines. Where Greathouse & Company had, in the spring of 1864, upped their service to a daily stage from Idaho City to Placerville.

The "stranger" (Alvy Boles) led the Asbills and the foot racer along the lower foothill pack trails north and crossed the Sacramento River near Red Bluff and probably took the trail to Peanut, Hayfork, Weaverville, Scott Valley and on to Humbug where they won big. It seems that Pierce may have stayed on for awhile.

Also we know from Markham's life story that while herding sheep he met a man on the trail in the Asbill areas of Mendocino Co. in the 1870's who offered him a job. When Markham saw Black Bart's pictures in the 1883 papers of course he called him Charles Bolton, as that was how Bart was identified in the papers. And that is the name by which he was imprisoned and what everyone called him. In 1883 Bart was going to San Quentin and Markham had no reason to disclose how long he and his family had known Joaquin Miller, Black Bart (aka Alvy Boles), or members of the Asbill family.

Pierce and Frank Asbill, no different than anyone else of that time, knew most probably long before seeing his picture in the papers, that Alvy Boles was Black Bart. And Pierce's son Frank, born in 1883, would have been only told about Bart as being the stranger from San Francisco who spent time at the White's ranch hunting butterflies. So Frank Asbill who wrote *The Last of the West* had no reason to suspect that the stranger he had heard about his father meeting in Placerville in 1864 was the same stranger at his dinner table in the 1870's.

And young Frank Asbill remembered Pierce's story this way:

"In the later seventies a preacher came up on his saddle horse and then came a sheriff and a beef buyer and "about this time a good looking fella came along the fence which ran west of the barn which was the fence to the field in the meadow. As he came along he threw a few rocks at some scampering squirrels. When he came to the house he stepped up on the porch, removed his hat and bowed to the *Wylackie* squaw [woman] who invited him inside. The room he entered was a large, inviting place. He turned towards the squaw and asked, "Is Pierce Asbill home?

The squaw answered, 'He go Covelo, get sheep shearers. He go [like] hell way he come back same way.'

The stranger seated himself on a rawhide bottom chair, saying he would wait. Pierce returned and entered the living room where the stranger sat. The stranger had the quick movements of a panther, much in contrast to the mountain men. And because of this,

Perce knew instantly who he was... [Their old friend "The Packer."]

At that moment the crooked cowhorn blasted for dinner. Everybody washed up in the long water trough

at the back of the house where the long roller-towel hung. The preacher, the sheriff, and the cow buyer all came in through the back door. Pierce, Frank, and the stranger came in from the living room. They all took their places at the table.

Pierce knew the three men and greeted them with the 'Hi-air Hi-air'ye be seated. Jen' tel'men, just be seated.' But he didn't introduce the stranger. This was not good western manners, especially among that gathering of men from such different walks of life.

But this procedure was not unusual for Pierce or for

Frank either. They never talked much and the stranger they knew was Charles Bolton, alias—"Black Bart"— the lone bandit that fiction thrives on today. [Frank Asbill errs as his father knew Black Bart as Bolton but knew his guest as Alvy Boles and didn't know his connection until Bart was later caught and his picture was in the papers.]

After all were seated at the long table where the squaws had piled the steaming food the men pitched in.

It consisted of fat buck steak, milk gravy, spuds with the skins on, and buckeroo beans [beans, brown sugar, garlic, barbecue sauce or mixed spices, left over ham or ground beef, and chopped up bacon]. And of course there was always bacon and eggs. Most mountain men ate bacon and eggs as often as they could get them.

Pierce sat at one end of the table while Frank sat at the other. The stranger sat to Pierce's left, the sheriff of Mendocino County sat to his right, just across the table from the stranger. The stranger eyed the sheriff sharply and asked him whether he had captured the bandit who had robbed the Overland Stage at Wool Rock? Wool Rock is just at the top of the hill going south from Willits, Mendocino County, California. This is where the highway turns down the Walker Valley grade.

The lawman, toting the star of authority said no but his men were on the bandits trail and he was expecting news at any time, of his capture. [The sheriff was probably still A.W. Montgomery who lived in Ukiah Twp., at the time of the 1870 census.]

The stranger spoke up, saying, 'That bandit is a cagey sort of fella!'

The sheriff laughed, saying: 'He sure will be when we get him caged.'

Pierce and Frank flashed a glance at each other.

That was all.

That night, Pierce put the stranger and the preacher in the same bed. And many years later I heard him say: 'By-gad, if 'em that er preacher would awoke to the fact that he was a sleepin' with that er Black Bart, that bandit, he'd a done some tall prayin', I'll betch'a!'" (*The Last of the West* pg.124-126).

Of course Frank Asbill (b.1883) on hearing this story would have had no way of knowing that when his father spoke of the "cattle buyer "that Pierce Asbill could have been referring to L.H. Gruwell who had moved to Lower Lake in Lake Co. around 1874 with his second wife, J.T. McClintock's daughter. When only 18,

L.H. Gruwell had come with his parents to Los Angeles, CA in the spring of 1849 and Laban was mining in the Louisville area of El Dorado Co. in 1850 while Alvy Boles was mining near Placerville in the same county.

When only 21 in 1857, L.H. Gruwell started speculating in stock buying (buying and selling cattle) for himself in Lake Co. And in 1861 he bought a ranch in Mendocino Co. but sold it in 1863. He then moved back to Lake Co. and married the daughter of a judge, then moved to Stoney Creek, Colusa Co. in 1866. His then moved on to a part of Siskiyou Co. [now Modoc] where his first wife had died in 1873. (*History of Napa and Lake Counties 1881*, Slocum, Bowen & Co. Publishers, 1881, p.237-238.)

L.H. Gruwell the stock speculator/buyer/raiser drove cattle to markets as far off as San Francisco and in 1872 he was living literally, in the same town as our miner -pack train operator –builder- lumber mill man, Alvy Boles. When Boles in 1872 was beaten up by two brothers, reported as the Bakers brothers or Black brothers in different papers. Shortly thereafter Gruwell's wife died and he returned to Lake County. There Gruwell had a farm and a livery stable and was said by relatives to have owned the stage and was driving it when Bart robbed it. But we have found no proof. Gruwell served as Supervisor for three months and was elected to that position in 1880. He was involved in the Lake County Agricultural Committee. Could he have been that cattle-buyer dinner guest at Asbill's table in 1878? You decide!

If the cattle buyer was Gruwell remember he was in Fall River Valley in 1872 when Boles was beaten by 2 brothers. Possibly the Baker Brothers as John Baker was hung in Shasta in 1874 for robbing and Murdering mail carrier George Cline who was delivering tax money from Fall River Mills to Shasta. Thus Gruwell would have known Alvy Boles before and after he was beaten up.

Chapter 11

Miller Returns

1872 is remembered by California historians as the year The Bohemian Club was founded in San Francisco by members of the working press. Charter members included Edward Bosqui, a prominent San Francisco publisher and Joaquin Miller (Joan Didion *Where I was From Alfred A. Knoff* 2003 p.83-84). Both men had a long history of ties to the Upper McCloud River area of Siskiyou Co.

Joaquin Miller probably read all that about his friend Alvy Boles as Miller was back in California and Oregon and he lectured Feb. 7 in San Francisco (*Sacramento Daily Union* Jan 1, 1873). So he surely would have heard of the aforementioned beating of Alvy Boles by two brothers.

We know, Joaquin Miller knew Alvy Boles well from 1853/54 on. And logically would have also known Alvy's son E. A. Boles. E.A. Boles had come west arriving by ship in San Francisco in June of 1853 and possibly joining Alvy in Yreka a full year before Miller arrived Yreka in late 1854.

In 1879 there was no Alvy Boles in the Siskiyou Co., CA Great Register and no longer was his son E. A. Boles with the Davidsons in Scott Valley. Records show that on Mar. 30 E. A. Boles (II) was born to E. A. Boles (I) in Genoa, Nevada where Emery (I) had a blacksmith and wagon making shop. But he also evidently had interests or property in Placerville, as his son was buried there in 1949.

And in 2011 Alvy's great, great grandson Dave Lee Boles went looking for him on the Internet:

"Grandfather related stories to my Dad about a man who would come into the family home after dark and leave before dawn. This was when my grandfather was young and living in Genoa, NV. He believed in later years that the mystery man was Black Bart. I haven't been able to find a link to Charles Everett Boles as of this date." (DB) The only connection..."My grandfather was Emery Allison. Boles II. His father was Emery Allison Boles I. I know my grandfather was born in Genoa, Nevada 3/30/1879 and married Amy Mary Wood (my grandmother), his second marriage. They lived in Santa Rosa CA, San Francisco, and Placerville, CA. My father, Leland Woodrow Boles, was born 7/13/1916 in Santa Rosa. He spent his early youth in San Francisco. He graduated from El Dorado High School in Placerville CA in 1935 [while probably living with his grandparents]. [And in answer to another query, Dave wrote]... "This information may be too far removed from what you are looking for. I have limited info on the Boles tree. I would like to know more about a Black Bart....

My grandfather said, that when Boles was arrested he said they could call him Charles E, Boles or Charles Bolton or whatever they liked. But eventually his picture appeared in print and everyone recognized him as the Alvy Boles they had known at some earlier period in their own lives. But no one chose to ever publicly identify the man while he was serving his time in San Quentin or ever thereafter. (David Lee Boles)."

Not even Charles Edwin Anson Markham ever used Black Bart's real name. He merely spoke of having met a man in the forests of Mendocino Co But he had to have known the family well for according to Wikipedia contributors Markham "taught literature in El Dorado Co. until 1879, when he became education superintendent of the county." While residing in El Dorado Co. Markham became a member of the Placerville Masonic Lodge. "Charles [Edwin] also accepted a job as principal of Tompkins Observation School in Oakland, California in 1890. "While in Oakland, he became well acquainted with many other famous contemporary writers and poets, such as Joaquin Miller, Ina Coolbrith, Charles Warren Stoddard, and Edmund Clarence Stedman."

You know they err in part, because Joaquin Miller's family and Markham's family first became acquainted in Oregon in 1852 and Edwin Markham in Placerville had to have known the Boles family in 1880's as Emery Allison Boles was also a Mason there at that same time. And we know that in 1888 that Miller had written from his "Hights" to Edwin in Placerville to "attract a sympathetic and muscular workmate to his hillside." Edwin did move to Oakland and three years later moved to "within a half mile of the Hights. There he produced "ManWith the Hoe" one of the most popular and lucrative poems of all times." (Phoebe Cutler "Joaquin Miller and the Social Circle at the Hights." CALFORNIA HISTORY. *The Journal of the California Historical Society.* Vol. 90, No.1, 2012 p. 54)

Chapter 12

The Alva (Alvy) Boles Family

Today's cold dispassionate census data provides our only "clewes" to the story of Alvy's lineage or to the personal tragedy in his life which made his story different from many other California gold seekers of his day.

Like many Americans Alvy Boles' ancestors evidently came from England and possibly were descendants of Cornish miners. Further back than that I, Margaret Guilford-Kardell now 96 years old, will leave to younger "clewe" followers the teasing out of further verification.

One could possibly trace our Gold Rush Alvy Boles b. 1811 with 8 siblings including John K. b. 1802 through their Father Samuel Boles b.1779 PA.

According to *The Argonauts of California* (p.484) we know that an A. [Alva, Alvy?] Boles arrived by the schooner *Edward L. Frost* Nov 7, 1849 in San Francisco CA...And the census had him mining in Calaveras Co. (aka. Calaveras Dist.) in 1850.

And only four years later Alvy's son Emery Allison Boles, b. Apr. 15, 1841 in Brimfield, Portage Co. OH arrived in June of 1853 in San Francisco. Arriving on this same ship is Mrs. J.S. Emery who was joining her husband already in the gold fields, while 12 year old Emery Allison Boles joined his father, Alvy Boles, in Yreka.

And how coincidental is it that J.S. Emery's gold fortune built his home and orchards in sunny Fruitvale, CA and Joaquin Miller called himself an orchardist, and built his "Hights" (now Joaquin Miller Park) on Oakland's nearby fog covered hills that did not produce fruit so well. But it was where Frémont had camped when first in the area. Remember Hulings Miller had read Frémont's reports to the family back in Indiana before they even started for Oregon and Joaquin was just the child, Cinncinatus Hiner Miller.

And so was it just coincidence that Joaquin's mother was a celebrated guest at the Fruitvale Old Timers reunions. Margaret Miller was so proud of her son's accomplishments and celebrity. Perhaps even she knows that Joaquin Miller and J.S. Emery both had Liberty Ships named after them in WWII.

But, back to the tragedy in the life of Alvy Boles. Like most gold seeking 49'ers he probably intended to take his fortune back East where the twinkly eyed love of his life Dorcas was giving birth to his last son J. W. in 1850. In the later censuses Alvy began listing himself as a widower.

Dorcas herself ended up dying listed as Dorcas Boles Gordon.

Thus Alvy Boles, unlike other 49ers, as far as we know, did not <u>choose</u> to never return East but circumstantially decided to live out the rest of his life single in California. Although many of his closest mining friends and companions had Indian wives.

I do find *Karuk* Indians named Boles living near his old mine off of the Klamath River but so far have found no blood connection. But Alvy Boles did sell his place on Fall River in 1865 to Burgette who had an Indian wife, from where I do not know. But Boles had probably met Burgette in Silver City, Idaho around 1863 or 1864.

James Brock with whom Alvy often stayed when on the Pit River, had a *Wintu* Indian wife who had also been earlier, according to legend, the wife of Joaquin Miller and mother of Miller's so-called daughter Calle Shasta. And lastly, William Himes with whom Alvy Boles lived in 1880 in Fall River City evidently had a white wife.

So who was this Alvy Boles born 1811 according to later lost tombstone data and according to census and other records b. 1811/12/14, and thus in 1885 he would have been 71, 73, or 74. The 1880 census records lists Alvy Boles age 66, blacksmith, b. ca.1814, lived in the house of William Himes Twp. 4, Shasta Co. [In 1942 a William H, Himes (b.1880) was a bartender at Big Bend, on the Pit River]. Also according to 1880 Sept. 16, CA voter registration Alvy was also 68 but b. ca. 1812. [1880 Census data was obviously given by Himes not by Alvy. For in the 1850 census Alvy b. ca. 1812, by which he would have been 73 not 71 in 1885]. In 1880 no Boles in Siskiyou Co. Great Register.

In 1878 a Mary Vollmer supposedly had a liaison with Black Bart in Oroville, but she could have been a grown daughter visiting from the East under an assumed name. Nothing has been proven on her.

But obviously the blacksmith. William H. Himes, had known Alvy Boles for a long time, for Himes had been listed as registering to vote in Burgetteville (now Glenburn), Shasta Co. in 1873 and Alvy Boles had been off and on back in Fall River Valley since before the Massacre of 1856/57.

By 1880 Boles was again back in Fall River Valley, although he then evidently had three sons living in Nevada. The 1880 Census listed E.A. [Emery Allison] Boles b. OH 1839, as living in Genoa, Douglas Co. Nevada with wife Caroline (33 so b.1847) and son Ernest [aka. Emery Allison], and two boarders. Emery Allison Boles had been in Yreka in 1860 and Scott Valley in 1864 both places in Siskiyou County.

Recently, for sale on the Internet I found advertised an April 8,

1880 bill of sale by E.A. Boles, a Blacksmith and Wagon maker in Genoa, Douglas County, Nevada.

Also in Douglas Co. in Carson Valley, the 1880 Census listed J.W. Boles age 30 so b. 1850, in Wisconsin, living with A.B. Boles b. 1839. So J.W. Boles was possibly Alvy's youngest and last son.

This A. B. Boles, age 41, b. abt. 1839 also in Wisconsin, with his Father born in OH and his Mother b. PA. had also living with him and his wife and small children a J.W. Boles age 30 so born about 1850.

In 1880 the Census captured C.E. Bolton b. abt. 1834 in England, as living in San Francisco with 11 other men. Obviously neither this Bolton nor C. E. Boles were Alvy Boles, the real Black Bart.

Unfortunately, neither Bill O'Reilly's "Legends and Lies" 2016, nor the Jan. 22nd 2017 "Mysteries at the Museum" Hollywood version of Black Bart have the real Black Bart. Many of the legendary stories have been built on Black Bart being afraid of horses, and yet he was a blacksmith?

Too numerous to mention are the various versions of the Black Bart story. Such as 2009 Gail L. Jenner and Lou Legerton "Black Bart the Poet Bandit". And Lou Legerton was an ex-Wells Fargo public relations officer? Go figure.

Chapter 13

The London Celebrity Returns and Black Bart's Celebrity Begins

In 1875 Joaquin Miller was back in America and again writing his popular travelogues. A *St. Louis Globe Democrat* (June 28th) article of his was sub-titled "How the Quaker city looks to the Untamed Poet of the Western Wilds."

Obviously Miller was still promoting his "untamed" image even though he had just returned from London and had been to Italy, Palestine, Jerusalem, etc.

On returning to New York, Miller was very flip with some young reporters and claimed that "A ship of the desert was a camel." And that he was going to go to Arabia and would write "The Ship in the Desert." And when queried about having been in Nicaragua with Walker he replied; "Was Milton ever in hell?"

Miller went on from NY to visit one of his publishers Frank Fields at Saratoga Springs, where Field's wife the fabled Miriam continued Miller's celebrity education. She was rumored to have $70,000.00 in diamond jewelry and was the center of attention on any hotel veranda. Miriam instructed Miller to enter the veranda at the far end and walk slowly to their place at the other end.

It is unlikely that Miller while, at Saratoga Springs even read in the newspapers about some bandit dubbed by journalists "Black

Bart." He had robbed supposedly yet another California stage running from Sonora to Milton July 26, 1875. Actually it was only Bart's first robbery according to later records. And Miller would have had no reason for believing he knew the robber.

The same would have applied to Edward Markham who was in 1875 living in Placerville, CA with his first wife. Later Edwin Markham talked about having dug up gold hidden by Black Bart on his mother's ranch in Solano Co. But maybe Markham just borrowed that name for another robber he knew as that was back in 1868 that Markham dug up the gold that helped him through school and Bart didn't start robbing stages until 1875.

Chapter 14

Black Bard becomes Black Bart

═══════════════════════════════════

If you have never before read anything about stage robbers and stage coaches see Collins and Levene's 1992 *Black Bart.*

The question before us here is; Why Alvy Boles, the blacksmith, poet, gold miner, pack train operator, farmer, builder, father of six (?) and friend to both the Masons and the Indians, only became Black Bart after he was 64 years of age? Was it because he had suffered severe financial loss in Yreka's 1871 fire and was nearly beaten to death by 2 brothers in 1873?

We know nothing of Alvy's activities 1873 to 1875. Perhaps Alvy had done some recuperating from the beating by living with his sons in Douglas Co. Nevada. Perhaps on his way back north when he started his retirement career by robbing a stage in the very Gold Rush area that had lured him to California in 1850.

Having walked beside his pack trains for the past 23 years he knew well the original Indian trails and the stage coach routes that followed. And having been an itinerant blacksmith he knew all the stage stops and no doubt personally, some of the drivers.

Black Bart knew well the sites of all of his future robberies and his potential escape routes as he had mined, packed, worked or lived near all of them. As the 1850 census had placed Alvy Boles mining in Calaveras Co. So it is no surprise that his first robbery was near Funk Hill in Calaveras Co. in July of 1875. And this was about 60 miles "as the crow flies," from where his son Emery Allison Boles lived in Genoa, Douglas Co. NV in 1870.

Bart's first cluster of robberies began on July 26, 1875, and ended with his last (29th Nov. 3, 1883). It includes one sort of an en-route robbery and puts him travelling through, and or living in Amador, Calaveras, and Tuolumne Cos. where he had first prospected upon arriving in California.

All four robbery clusters have a North to South axis. For example cluster number one's northernmost robbery, which was robbery number 28, occurred at Morrow Grade. Four miles from Jackson and only about 36 miles "as the crow flies" from his southernmost robbery which was robbery number 1.

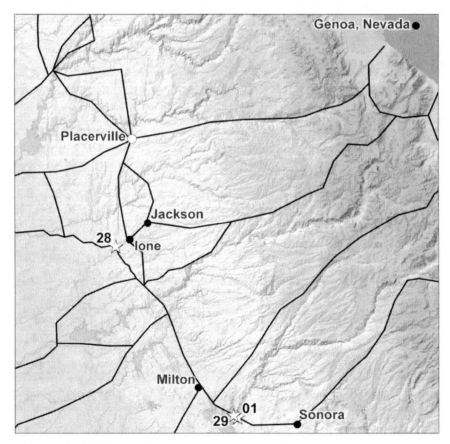

Robbery cluster map with # 1, 28, 29

Bart's second cluster began with robbery number 2 and ends with number 24. The the northernmost robbery in this cluster is number 6 about 30 miles (as the crow flies) from robbery number 2 near Smartsville.

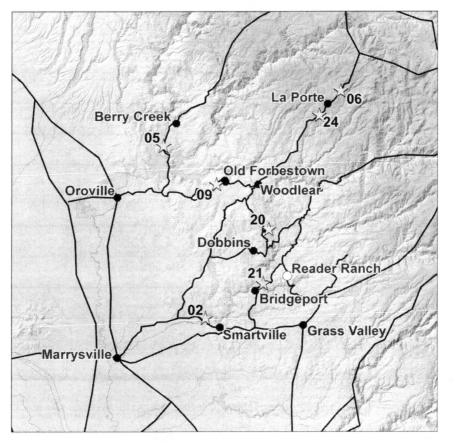

Robbery cluster map with # 2, 5, 6...

Bart's third cluster begins with number 3 in Oregon and ends with number 25. The northernmost robbery is number 15 and was about 105 miles "as the crow flies" from the southernmost robbery number 11. This was also the cluster in which he had, during his lifetime, the greatest number of abodes and friends.

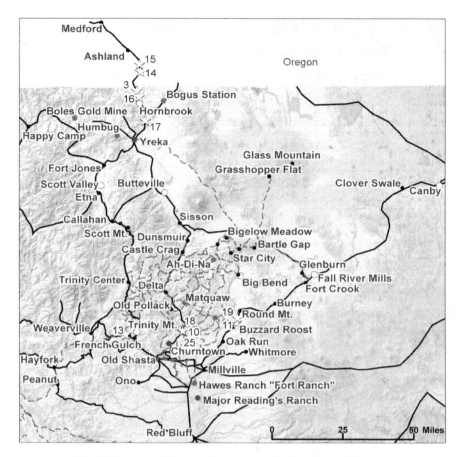

Robbery Map cluster # 3, 10, 11,....

Bart's fourth and last cluster begins with number 4 and ends with number 27. The northernmost robberies numbers 7, 8, and 23 were all about 30 miles "as the crow flies" from the southernmost robberies, numbers 4 and 12.

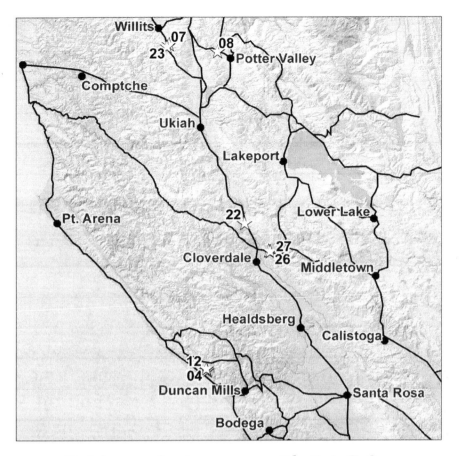

Robbery cluster map with # 4, 7, 8...

So it would seem that he tried first; one robbery in each area in which he had prior knowledge, residence or work. Subsequent robberies in each cluster, perhaps, were then decided on a basis of need, opportunity, and relevance to other work opportunities, and probably more often because of where his friends lived.

Chapter 15

History Coalesces

Robbery No.1

Basically we only need to know here for our exploration of the life of the Real Black Bart, Alvy Boles, that; John Shine, the stage driver left Sonora at 3 a.m. headed for Milton and the stage was robbed at Funk Hill, four miles east of Copperopolis in Calaveras Co., July 26, 1875.

Of course early accounts included all sorts of guesstimates and fabrications-many fostered by Bart pretending to be a tramp and asking for food and directions when all the time he knew exactly where he was. But we know nothing further of Bart's activities during 1875 until his after Christmas robbery Dec. 28, 1875 in Yuba Co.

Black Bart, having lived on stage routes since their beginnings in the west knew all about the drivers, the routes and the equipment. This documented in Bruce Levenes account of the robberies "Black Bart" Pgs. 19-148. So it is not difficult to presume that after visiting with family and friends for Christmas in Douglas Co. Nevada, that on his way back north he took the opportunity to replenish his purse by robbing the North San Juan to Marysville stage December 28, 1875 in Yuba County, four miles from Smartsville.

Robbery No. 2

Our robbery cluster map shows robberies 2, 5, 6, 9, 20, 21, and 24 in Butte, Nevada, Plumas, and Yuba Cos in California. Others postulated that perhaps Bart didn't commit either of the two robberies reported at that time in Yuba Co. But they gave us a complete description of robbery number 2 and credited Bart with the San Juan to Marysville stage just four miles from Smartsville.

In his second cluster of robberies, no doubt, Alvy Boles and his pack mules had traveled all the trails that had become stage routes. He was, so to speak, in his own territory.

We have no knowledge of Alvy Boles whereabouts earlier in 1875. But we do know that from a San Francisco friend, Miller learned that Hill Beachy, from Miller and Alvy Boles's Idaho days, had died. Before, when all been in Idaho, Beachy had been the sheriff in Boise, who had captured the killers of the Magruder party. Miller had reported for the papers about those times in Idaho and about his fellow miners from his Shasta and Siskiyou days.

Alvy Boles, like Miller, was an avid reader of news about the places they had lived and mined. News of Beachy's death would have carried Alvy back to 1868, when he read, probably in Shasta Co. The news Miller was reading in Portland in 1868, of "The Marion More Tragedy." Marion More, of the Ida Elmore mine, was killed in a shoot-out with Sam Lockhart in front of the Idaho Hotel, Owyhee County, Idaho. Hill Beachy, a part owner in The Golden Chariot Mine saved Sam Lockhart for jail and death three months later (13th of July). Lockhart and Beachy had known each other since those first Shasta mining days. Lockhart may also have been a partner in The Golden Chariot. Hill Beachey as well as George Grayson and George Hearst had an interest in the Golden Chariot Mine on War Eagle Mountain right next to the Ida Elmore mine.

According to some, George Hearst was often in and out of Silver City.

Back in the 1860's not many kept records and by late 1864 most folks like Miller and Boles had left Rocky Bar, Idaho. Only recently have the pictures surfaced from Idaho archives of Boles and others mentioned in Miller's 1864 article about Rocky Bar which you read on earlier pages herein.

One wonders if Waldo Elmore had been there too and did he have a connection to the Ida Elmore mine. Because Waldo Elmore who had arrived in California in 1852 and mined in Shasta Co. and who also became a secretary for many mining companies. But he didn't marry Lucinda until late 1863 or early 1864 as their first child was born Aug. 19, 1864. Lucinda was the daughter of Chief *Num-te-ra-re-man*, a signer of the 1851 Indian Treaty at Maj. Reading's Ranch. This Indian Chief was head of the Cow Creek Indians. In *Wintu,* Cow Creek was *Puidalpom Puiwakat* (Easterly place East Entering Creek*)* and that is the creek that more or less parallels the Pit River at the crossing to Brock Creek.

Miller also learned on his 1875 visit back to the States that his friend and distant relative James R. Keene had been made president of the San Francisco Stock and Exchange Board. And by September Ambrose Bierce (born on 24 June 1842) was also again back in San Francisco.

And from the Yreka papers Miller learned that Lieutenant General Phil. Sheridan and his brother Col. Sheridan, with their wives, had arrived on a special six-horse stage, Sept. 15/75. M. Miner, Yreka merchant and cousin of the Sheridans, had met the stage at Shasta River and accompanied the honored guests to their hotel.

Miller remembered that Sheridan had served at Fort Reading before Miller ever mined in Shasta County and had also done some surveying in the Willamette Valley, Oregon after Miller had left only a year before in 1854.

Miller also had read about some old timers he knew who were also visiting Yreka, like Stephen Meek (brother of Oregon's Joe Meek) who evidently returned to Scott Valley near the Glendening Brother's home. Meek had first seen Scott Valley in 1833when he accompanied Walker, who was detached from Capt. Bonneville's party then exploring the Rocky Mountains. Again in 1842 Meek had passed through Scott Valley with Tom McKay, father of Donald McKay. On June 20, Joe Meek died and was buried two days later on his farm four miles north of Hillsboro, Oregon. He had been born in Washington Co. Virginia and now he was buried in Washington Co. Oregon. Just as Miller's kin John Miller Sr., born in Carter, Tennessee and married to Mary Keene, had been buried in Linn Co. O. T., in 1858 and later joined in death with his kin George Miller Sr. buried in 1874 in Millersburg Cemetery in Linn Co. OR just north of the Hulings Miller Lane Co., OR farm. How typical of the treks of so many of the families of that time.

According to some historians, expatriates like Miller, while in London, spent all their time with Oscar Wilde - just out of Oxford, and James Whistler languishing at "the feet of Lily Langtry." Miller, for one, was also busy writing and penning letters to his "dear Charley" [Charles Warren Stoddard] and others. And he was also often meeting with other poets like the night that Watts [Thomas Watts-Dunston 1832-1914] had to his rooms Swinburne [Algernon Charles Swinburne 1837-1909], Gosse [Edmund 1849-1928], Minto [William Minto 1846-1893], Scottish critic and Professor of Logic and English at the University of Aberdeen], Rossetti [Dante Gabriel Rossetti 1828-1882] and Miller, to hear Thomas Gordon Hake, an English physician turned poet after retirement, whose poetry was admired by the Rossettis. Miller then and there was learning from some of the best minds of that time.

Miller also got together with an alert actor who helped him put together "The First Woman in the Forks" and "The Last Man of Mexican Camp" as a play called "The First Families in the Sierras" published in 1875 in London by George Routlege & Sons. .

Then Miller put it into book form and published it in London and in 1876 in Chicago with Jansen, McClurg and Company. The story was about a young woman disguised as a man who hides out from religious assassins at a mining camp called the Forks. The Forks was near Humbug Creek, near Yreka. Much of the book takes place at the "Howling Wilderness" saloon. Mount Shasta was not mentioned per se, but much of the descriptive material was similar to that found in Miller's novel *Unwritten History: Life Amongst the Modocs.*

Miller's *The Ship in the Desert* came out in London as 140 pages under Chapman & Hall while the Boston edition by Roberts Bros. had 205 pages. It had a copyright 1875 by C.H. Miller and Miller signed the preface "Joaquin Miller Lake Como, Italy." Some lines that he hoped would be quoted for centuries:

> I saw the lightning's gleaming rod
> > Reach forth and write upon the sky
> > > The awful autograph of God.
> The very clouds have wept and died
> > And only God is in the sky.

In Mt. Shasta City there is a plaque on Mt. Shasta Blvd. where there is an unobstructed view of the mountain and it reads:

> Lonely as God and white as the winter moon.

On the building right next to the plaque is a mural with the mountain and Joaquin Miller, and the quote is there also.

Upon returning to New York and on being interviewed by some young reporters Miller claimed that "A ship of the desert was a camel." And that he was going to go to Arabia and would write "The Ship in the Desert."

And when queried about having been in Nicaragua with Walker Miller replied; "Was Milton ever in hell?"

So Miller being back in the states surely read about some California bandit by the name of Black Bart who had started robbing stages: Sonora to Milton July 26, and San Juan to Marysville Dec. 28/75. And Edwin Markham talked about having dug up gold hidden by Black Bart on his mother's ranch. But maybe he just borrowed that name to cover another robber he knew as it was back in 1868 that Markham supposedly dug up the gold that helped put him through school and the Black Bart robberies didn't start until 1875.

And Miller probably never knew that was the year Dorcas Boles Gordon died back east and a daughter of Dorcas Boles married. And Alva Boles, possibly a son of the Alvy Boles he knew from his Siskiyou and Idaho days had also married. Miller probably didn't know any of this and wouldn't have connected any such information to his old friend Alvy Boles at that time, and certainly not to any robberies.

Chapter 16

Robbery No. 3

Our third cluster map obviously starts with robbery number 3 but also includes 10, 11, 13, 14, 15, 16, 17, 18, 19, and 25 all in Northernmost California and just over the line in Oregon. And all obviously on Indian trails which later became stage coach routes. First Alvy Boles in 1850 and later Joaquin Miller in 1854 began their notorious days living there centered around Yreka in Siskiyou Co., and Redding, Fall River Valley in Shasta and Modoc Cos. Their true history is still being uncovered there today.

Back in 1876 Miller was a success at 37 while 65 year old Alvy Boles's funds from his Dec. 28, 1875 robbery were evidently expended and he learned of a granddaughter, Idah May Boles, being born 15 May 1876 in Carson City, Nevada. So, June 2, 1876 found Bart committing his third robbery.

This time just five miles north of Siskiyou Co.'s town then called Cottonwood, but now called Hornbrook. Collins and Levene report of this robbery said it was just two miles south of the California and Oregon border.

Now Hornbrook is only about 15 miles from Bogus where today the Copco Dam is located on the Klamath River. And in Bogus in1875 a resident farmer/wool grower also postmaster, was a .W.K McClintock also kin to the new wife of Alvy Boles's cattle buying friend and neighbor, L.H Gruwell from Alvy's most recent 1872 Fall River Mills days.

As usual, had the detectives realized that Bart had local connections they could have easily tracked him further on from his tracks on Hutton Creek on East only 15 or so miles up the Klamath River to McClintock's place at Bogus.

Alvy Boles also could have canoed from Hutton Creek down the Klamath River and/or used pack trails toward Humbug and turned off at Horse Creek and gone 3.2 miles north to his mine.

As usual he simply disappeared into plain sight. His options were endless. And Yreka was also close by.

Chapter 17

The Reader Ranch

Bart's take hadn't been great but it evidently provided enough stage fare to get him back down to Nevada Co. CA where he found work near his earlier 2nd robbery site and near his sons in Douglas Co. NV.

Various accounts tell us it was the summer 1876 that a "Mr. Martin" [Alvy Boles] appeared at the Reader Ranch on Shady Creek near Nevada City in Nevada Co. CA. There he worked for a month or so at the sawmill on the ranch, then moved on only to return periodically for a month or so in spring or fall. Remember Alvy had had sawmills before, first in Edgewood and then in Fall River Mills.

Bart's second robbery Dec. 28, 1875 had been only five miles south and west of the Reader Ranch and Frank Reader identified the spot ..." at a rock turn 0.8 miles south and upgrade from the Bridgeport covered bridge. Frank, as a boy, remembered hearing this story here repeated by his grandson Greg Watkins. "It was raining hard the day of the robbery, and a county road maintenance man was working his way along the road turning off the water from the road ruts with a shovel. (This shovel work would prevent the storm from eroding deep gullies in the road.) He was wearing a rain slicker as he came around the corner upon the stage robbery in progress the robber saw the man and commanded him to lay flat on the road and to pull the slicker over his head and not to look up. The maintenance man said he laid there a long time afraid to get up. Perhaps the robber ordered him into the stage at the end of the robbery when he ordered the stage to "Get going!"

Mr. Martin always walked to and from the ranch and never carried a gun, And one time Martin loaned Jim Reader $300.00 in gold coins so Jim wouldn't have to ride into town in a storm to collect debts owed him so he could pay the mill workers.

"Martin" [Alvy Boles] may have been familiar with the name Reader as there were Readers in Trumbell Co. OH where Alvy Boles' parents were married.

Chapter 18

Homeward Bound

Was Alvy Boles celebrating the birth of another grandchild Harry or Henry Elsworth Boles b.11 July, 1877 in Genoa Nevada, or was he just visiting old friends on the coast on his way back north when he committed his fourth robbery Aug. 3, 1877 in Sonoma Co. The stage from Point Arena to Duncan's Mills, at a point 4 miles from Fort Ross at the top of Myers Grade

This robbery became famous because of a note left with a poem on a tree stump this note included the words ... "to our friend, the other driver." Psychiatrists today might suggest that this meant that Bart might have known the earlier driver he had just robbed. That was possible.

For in 1851 a Marshall Cummings was the first stage driver to drive a Baxter & Monroe coach north from Colusa to Monroeville, Red Bluff, Cottonwood, Horsetown, Middletown, and lastly to Shasta. And years later in Mendocino Co. there was a Cummings Stage Station located 13 ½ miles from Laytonville on the Humboldt Rd. in Mendocino Co. (*History of Mendocino and Lake Cos.*)

Another Cummings, J.S., had been well known to Alvy Boles and everyone else in Yreka, until 1857 when he left. But by 1864 J.S. was living in Bodega, Sonoma Co. and was found in 1880 in Big Valley, Lake Co. probably with his son.

Now, it is only 28.4 miles from Fort Ross to Bodega in Sonoma Co. to where J.S. Cummings b. in North Carolina, lived from 1864 onward. It is only 13.3 miles by today's roads from Two Rock, Sonoma Co. to Bodega, in Sonoma Co. where there lived both the Asbill and Cummings, friends of Alvy Boles. Was he just visiting around?

Chapter 19

An Expensive Year

Bart must have had a great need for cash in 1878 for he committed three robberies that year. First was robbery number 5 on June 25, 1878 of the stage from Quincy to Oroville about a mile above Berry Creek.

This was the year that the Detective Hume began to put together that so many of the robberies were being made by the same robber. And Bart quickly followed with his sixth robbery July 30, 1878 by hitting the La Porte to Oroville stage at a point about six miles from La Porte.

For whom or where Black Bart worked or visited from August to October of 1878 we can't be quite sure, but he did end up pulling off back to back robberies in Mendocino Co. Oct.2 and Oct. 3. First was his 7th The Cloverdale and Arcata stage traveling south after stops at Cahto, Laytonville and Willits, and was about ten miles from its next station, Ukiah, the county seat. And the next day was his 8th robbery, a few miles north of Centerville, near the junction with a wagon road that went east to Lake County, — the only time a stage was ever robbed on that route."

Now of course you and we now know Bart- as Alvy Boles- may have known the Asbills from the Mendocino area since their earliest mining days in El Dorado Co. around 1850 and more probably from when Pierce had been mining in Shasta Co. 1858-1860. And descendants suggest that it was after Oct. 2, 1878 robbery that the now famous dinner at the Asbill ranch took place.

Collins ad Levene's 1992 Black Bart colorfully covered both robberies and told us all about the frustrated Detective Hume. And by the time they had chronicled Bart's 7th and 8th robberies they had decided that ... ***Black Bart possessed superior endurance in hiking cross-country very difficult terrain. By the following day he had eluded the posse and was 20 miles due east.***

Now check your map and you will see that as the crow flies it is a few miles from a point ten miles north of Ukiah to the Asbill ranch and from the ranch a few miles north of Centerville which adds up to roughly 20 miles with an overnight stay at the Asbills.

The 1992 story has the sheriff tracking Bart ...east, following his trail over scrub-laden foothills to the Mountain House, twelve miles from Williams in Colusa County, where the trail went cold. Bart had disappeared, after hiking more than 70 miles in 48 hours. He probably boarded the Central Pacific Railroad at Williams and took the train to either Sacramento or the Bay area.

Chapter 20

1879 Back to Butte Co. and Shasta Co.

Saturday June 21, 1879 found Black Bart striking again in Butte Co. It was his 9ᵗʰ robbery and it was just three miles below Forbestown, the La Porte stage headed for Oroville. There is now a Black Bart Road there which goes from Forbestown Rd. to Forbestown Rd. (presumably a parallel road).

And you can speculate on which of his numerous stopping places he called home until he struck again for his tenth robbery but the most important in giving us our major "clewe"s in tracing his methods of operation. For this was his first Bass Hill robbery. Here he clearly used Indian trails some of which have become modern roads and others forever buried under Shasta Lake. The Bass Hill plaque commemorating stage drivers has moved many times since the 1879 October 25, Shasta County, Bass Hill robbery by Black Bart of the Oregon to Redding Stage en route to Buckeye. It was his largest haul to date $1,400.00. But they lost his trail within a mile of the Copper City Rd. So where did Bart go?

This robbery gave us two of our most important "clewe"s to the true identity of Black Bart. It was dark at night and the stage had just crossed the Pit River and was climbing south up Bass Hill when Bart struck just 100 yards from the top of Bass Hill. One of the passengers was a Mrs. Bigelow from Butteville [Edgewood] but she couldn't see him in the dark. However, later Mae Hazel Southen (first president of the Shasta Historical Society) wrote in her memoirs after she had seen Bart's pictures in the paper that Mrs. Bigelow should have recognized her sometimes neighbor. And of course the trackers lost him at the Copper City Rd. as they probably thought he had crossed back north across the Pit River. Actually all he had to do was continue easterly along the Indian's Backbone Ridge trail and then cross over to Brock's place from which he could easily walk to robbery number 11.

Robbery No.11

Obviously Bart didn't have far to go for his next robbery on Oct. 27, 1879 which was still in Shasta Co. This one was only twelve miles north from Millville; where Fern Rd. becomes Whitmore Rd. This time it was the stage from Alturas to Redding. All accounts give us great background but understandably missed the obvious, as did all the detectives in 1879. They thought at that time that Bart was the ex-Ohioan Frank Fox and they presumed he would have headed back south toward civilization with all his loot.

And, again Indian trackers supposedly lost Bart's trail. Lost? Hardly! Bart had probably returned to James Brock's cabin on Brock Creek on the Pit River. This is where earlier he had probably stayed for awhile after escaping the Fall River Valley Massacre of 1856/7.

This was the same Brock's cabin where Joaquin Miller and supposedly his Indian woman had been living with Brock while sometimes mining at Clear Creek. And from where, in 1859, Miller rode to Millville and Shasta, where he bought guns and ammunition for the Indians.

A look at our map of robberies 10 and 11 show how wrong the guesstimates were of those 1879 lawmen and journalists as to who Black Bart really was, and to where he was going after each and every robbery. These two robberies were not exceptions but followed a pattern. He robbed on stage coach routes near places he had lived or had walked with his pack mules on the Indian trails that preceded the stage coach routes. He didn't frequent hotels but stayed with relatives or old friends he was visiting. Between robberies he became again the Black Bard, the itinerant blacksmith poet.

Perhaps Bart tarried at Brock's place after Robbery 11 we don't know. He may have returned by Indian trails directly to either the Glenburn or Fall River Mills areas where he had lived. Or perhaps he went down to his sons' places in Nevada for the holidays. And it may have been that he registered himself Feb. 10, 1880 as Carlos E. Bolton staying at the Sperry and Perry Hotel in Murphy giving his address as Silver Mountain (Collins 1992, 213). Feb. 11 someone signed as C. E. Bolton, Silver Mountain.

Did Alvy perhaps return to the Reader Ranch in Nevada Co. for another stint at their sawmill operation? We don't know. But remember Bart did show up in the 1880 census as living with William Himes and family in Twp. 4, Shasta Co.

Chapter 21

Back in Sonoma Co.

It gets blistering hot in Shasta Co. in the summer and so July 22nd, 1880 found Black Bart down in Sonoma Co. robbing his 12th Stage. The one from Point Arena to Duncan's Mill, four miles South of Henry's station on the way to Duncan Mills. Same location as his robbery on August 3, 1877, and Wells Fargo added it to the list after Bart was captured causing numbering confusion in various reports thereafter. Collins and Levene's 1992 version came close when he reasoned that *the numerous coastal robberies were committed by someone quite familiar with the area*.

As we already know Bart, being really Alvy Boles, didn't have to use the train to get there as he could have been visiting with friends in the area. And since he was soon robbing another stage in Shasta Co. we know Bart didn't stay over for the Sept. 12, 1880 marriage of 45 year old Pierce Asbill to Katie A. Robertson (Some Asbill data from *History of Mendocino Co. California*, Alley, Bowen & Co. Publishers, San Francisco, California).

Robbery No. 13

Probably on Alvy's way back north to Yreka, only five weeks after robbery number 12 Alvy executed Robbery 13, on Sept. 1, 1880 in Shasta Co. on Trinity Mt. Two miles east of Last Chance

Sta., about 11 miles north of Tower House and 65 miles (as the crow flies) south from Yreka where Harry L. Wells was winding up his interviews of locals for his *History of Siskiyou County, California 1881.* It was presumed that Bart escaped to Eagle Creek near Ono; then down Cottonwood Creek Trail to Tehama Co., with his loot estimated at only about $113.00. But the accompanying maps show very well that Black Bart had numerous places nearby where he was simply known and accepted as Alvy Boles, the packer, or later as Alvy Boles, the itinerant blacksmith.

Collins and Levene's 1992 analysis gave us all the data available at the time but then no one had made the connection between the location "11 miles north of Tower House" as being connected to the story of the "Seven Mules" which Alvy Boles had evidently told Harry L. Wells in Yreka the same year, 1880. And no one connected the same "11 miles north of Tower House to the famous "Lost Cabin" stories first referred to by Joaquin Miller circa 1871 and popularized by Wells in 1883 just after Bart's capture. It is patently obvious that both Miller and Wells had first heard these stories from Alvy Boles.

As usual the pundits got it wrong on Bart's escape routes. He more likely traveled his old pack trails (by then the stage routes he was robbing) right on north around 65 miles to Yreka where he could daily feed Harry L. Wells the stories of the early 1850's and the gold rush days in Shasta and Siskiyou Cos. Or perhaps he had only to just stop along his way in Etna, Scott Valley, and or at Fort Jones to catch up with Wells still finishing off all his info-gathering on the various Davidson families. Boles would have been regaling them with all the news from down Mendocino way of those who had lived in Siskiyou Co. and of Portuguese Frank whom they had met back in everyone's 1860's Rocky Bar Idaho days.

Robbery 14

Obviously Alvy didn't tarry long in Scott Valley or Yreka and was probably, perhaps by way of Humbug and his mine on Horse Creek, visiting friends in the Hornbrook area from where he didn't have to go far north to commit his 14th robbery. This time in Jackson Co., Oregon on Thursday, September 16, 1880. It was another near midnight holdup and this time on the Siskiyou Summit just six miles north of the Oregon California border and still close to the site of his 3rd robbery.

Robbery No. 15.

As you now know, Bart knew numerous ranchers nearby where he could have visited or shoed horses for a few days. So it is no surprise that on the same day, as news reports of robbery number 14 hit the street, Bart struck again with robbery number 15 on Thursday, September 23, 1880 again in Jackson Co. Oregon

"As Nort Eddings was ascending the Siskiyou Mountains Thursday night he was stopped at the last turn near the summit by a road agent and ordered to deliver the mail. The highwayman emphasized his proclamation by the display of a dangerous looking gun, and Nort saw no other alternative than to obey. Having complied with this, the robber called upon him to throw out the express box, but upon being informed that it was fastened in the boot, commanded Nort to stand at the heads of the leaders while he knocked in the box with an ax he had previously secreted in the brush. Having secured his booty, with all the nonchalance possible, he informed Nort that he might now proceed. There was only one passenger aboard, a lady, and she was not molested. The express box contained gold-dust, etc. to the amount of about $1,000. Eddings was stopped near the same place last year and says he is getting tired of the sport" (Jacksonville (Oregon) *Democratic Times*).

Robbery No. 16

November 20, 1880 found Bart still in his original Shasta/ Siskiyou area and probably again working out of Yreka or Hornbrook. He committed his 16th robbery just a mile south of the Oregon border and this time held up a north bound stage. This time he got nothing but a terrible fright according to the 1992 ***Bruce Levene's*** full account of this misadventure. This didn't take into account for the fact that there was a Davidson and a McClintock living and working nearby.

My search for ""clewe"s" again led me to the 1880 U.S. Census and Harry L. Wells said to be living in Oakland but we know he had been getting stories from Alvy Boles in Yreka. So Boles probably had told his "Seven Mules Story" to Wells in Yreka between his 1880's robberies because Wells published it in the Nov. 27, 1880 *Yreka Journal.* It was all about a pack train excursion by Alvy in 1851 through territory adjacent to Bart's robbery number 13 in that same September of 1880. The following year, 1881, Harry L. Wells publishes *History of Siskiyou County, California 1881*. Publisher D.J. Stewart, Oakland CA. (Wells, 166) writes "There is still another noted robber, a mysterious character known as the Black Bard. His operations have extended from one end of the Pacific Coast the other" [sic Oregon border to Mendocino, Calaveras and El Dorado Cos.]

Also in 1881, Frank and Chappell's *History and Business Directory of Shasta County* referred to our Alvy Boles but only as Bowles p.21 and 132. They also referred to a James Dunn as a blacksmith at Burgettville. (p.158). Dunn had obviously replaced Burgette who bought out our Alvy Boles in 1865.

But in those days no one was weaving a story out of the "clewe"s. And we know nothing of Alvy Boles' or Black Bart's activities until May 7, 1881 announcement in the *Mountain Democrat,* Placerville, CA of the birth of a child April 28, 1881 to E.A. Boles and his wife in Genoa, NV. (DB)

Robbery No.17

Bart didn't strike again until Aug, 31, 1881 when he robbed the overland stage from Roseburg, Oregon bound via Jacksonville for Redding. It was again 1:30 A.M. but this time the stage was coming up Kelly grade from the Anderson ferry across the Klamath River, just ten miles north of Yreka, and John Sullaway was the driver.

There is absolutely no way that Alvy Boles could <u>not</u> have known who John Sullaway was as his father, William Sullaway, arrived in Siskiyou Co. in 1852 from Calaveras Co. just one year after Alvy. William first mined, then started an express wagon between Yreka and Hawkinsville, and was founder of the pioneer stage line from Yreka to Shasta via the Sacramento River in 1857. Pack mules still had to be used for the part from Soda Springs to Shasta. (*Siskiyou Co. History 1881 ibid p.* 208C.)

Robbery No. 18.

The papers thought robbing stages south of Yreka was harder than north of Yreka, but Bart was back in the Bass Hill area in Shasta Co. Saturday, Oct. 8, 1881. This time the robbery was "two miles out of Bass Station, sixteen miles north of Redding, on the Sacramento Rd. as it was then called. And the driver was Horace Williams-robbed twice by Bart. They had to have known each other in their everyday lives.

As usual there is the disastrous loss of tracks even after they find a discarded registered envelope. And guess what? They lost the track on the old trail that led to Copper City. Sound familiar? Sure enough, Bart was heading back easterly to Fall River Mills by way of Brock's place on the Pit River.

Robbery No. 19

Do see **Bruce Levene's** 1992 *Black Bart* for his full report on Brewster, the driver. But accounts vary as to the location of Robbery number 19, Tuesday, Oct. 11, 1881

There were no passengers on Brewster's stage when Bart struck again. Because the brake blocks (or possibly a piece of harness) on his stage had loosened, the driver was forced to pull up at Montgomery Creek, two miles from the Round Mountain post office (then known as Buzzard's Roost), about 20 miles from his [Brewster's] home. Near 2 p.m. he finished repairing the stage and was ready to climb back up on the box: A man dressed in a long linen duster buttoned close up under his chin, a flour sack over his head for a mask and feet wrapped up in sacks, stealthily stepped up behind him from the brush, and presenting his shot-gun said: 'You found me have you?'

Such a complete disguise was particularly necessary for Black Bart this time as Lewis L. Brewster, the driver, had his own stage station on Tamarac Rd. on the way east into Burney where Brewster became Constable in 1882. (Dottie Smith's Blog *Redding Record Searchlight* Nov. 31, 2012). Brewster claimed he knew well Mark Twain (Samuel Clemens) so he maybe also knew Joaquin Miller, as Miller also knew Twain well. But I leave more on all that to younger historians.

And we know Alvy Boles since, 1856/57 had been in and around the Fall River area. And he was headed back through this area.

We do know that when Brewster said the robbery was at Montgomery Creek he most probably meant the creek proper, not the Town. Which the stage road crossed on its westerly route after it had cleared today's town of Montgomery Creek. Longtime residents postulate that he wouldn't have stopped at noon to make a repair in a town then less than a block long.

This robbery was very uncharacteristic of Bart's operation He usually stopped stages as they had pulled up a long grade or were slowed by a tight curve. Here Brewster had made an unscheduled stop after a long downhill run and Bart had watched from the woods as Brewster made his repairs.

The various accounts do not say how much Bart gained from the robbery, if anything. However, later in the 1900's some teens did unearth on the old Buzzard Hotel site, what they thought was a lead bar which turned out to be silver. It could have been buried by many different people or even Black Bart at another time as he used that trail numerous times as it led to his other robbery clusters

Brewster did wonder if it wasn't the same robber who had done the Bass Hill robbery Oct. 8, just 2 days before. He evidently was dead right. From my research it would seem that after the Bass Hill robbery Bart had probably gone to Brock's place on the Pit River and by the 11th was continuing walking his way back home to Fall River Mills.

Back in 1881 when the detectives arrived and a posse was formed at Round Mountain [Buzzard's Roost] they thought they tracked Bart south nearly to Oroville. They also interviewed locals at Round Mountain who promised to report back, which they never did.

The locals may have known more than they were telling. We know that in 1881 Liepe Eilers was the blacksmith at Round Mountain (Frank and Chappell 1881 p. 167). And Joe Mazzini told me that in early days a Lu Eilers had a ranch, a store, a bar and a post office at Round Mountain. Lu also was the owner of the Grizzly Bear Claim and had much fire proof clay on his ranch (Frank and Chappell 1881 p.28). And D. Eilers was a farmer and store keeper at Fall River Mills. Remember, Alvy Boles often lived with the William H. Himes family when he was in Fall River Mills and Frank and Chappell have Himes listed as a farmer at Fall River Mills. (Frank and Chappel. Ibid 1881 p. 135). And the U.S. Census 1880 has Alvy Boles at Himes' Fall River Mills house.

Chapter 22

Robberies No. 20-28

The 20th Black Bart robbery was Dec. 15, 1881 about four miles above the Dobbins ranch (North 21 13 59 West) on the Downieville-Marysville run, Deputies found no tracks and according to the report there was no money in the box so he gained nothing.

Bruce Levene repeated the driver's account of Bart's unaccustomed use of swear words in this robbery.

Alvy Boles would have been familiar with the right place to stop a stage because on his earlier pack trains Alvy had undoubtedly picked up supplies. From Sacramento headed for Shasta City from 1853 onward. And Alvy had returned that way from his 1864 Idaho mining days.

So, if Alvy Boles had been planning to be a guest at either of his sons' homes in Douglas Co. Nevada for Christmas 1881 he would have had a 32 hour walk from the scene of the robbery to Reno NV and then a short stage ride or walk on down to Genoa.

Collins and Levene's 1992 closing comment on this robbery report is where they nailed Bart's *modus operandi*:

> **In the pursuit, like so many before him the deputy sheriff was no match for one of the best long-distance hikers since the ancient Greek, Phidippides of Marathon.**

Robbery No. 21

If accounts are correct Bart's 21st robbery, December 27, 1881 in Nevada County, at Bridgeport of the stage from North San Juan to Smartsville didn't pay. One account says Bart didn't get anything and another says "Nothing much taken," and Bart was also wrongly blamed for another stage robbery in Smartsville. But they did correctly guess that he had held up the Camptonville stage just before Christmas.

Robbery No. 22.

The 22nd robbery January 26, 1882 occurred in Mendocino County, six miles south of Cloverdale of the stage from Ukiah to Cloverdale. Again the posse is on his tracks within the hour and again they lose him after Kelseyville, on Clear Lake. (unknown E Boles was in Kelseyville census in 1878) Collis and Levene's 1992 version said the driver was Henry Forse going north from Cloverdale towards Hopland. The robbery occurred near the tollhouse. He obtained $300.00 from this robbery, so his luck had improved over the previous two robberies and he was again near friends and possibly doing a little mining in the area.

Robbery No. 23

Perhaps Bart stayed on in the area for he started his usual summer season with Robbery 23, on June 14, 1882, in Mendocino County The stage from Little Lake to Ukiah. A former County Supervisor Hiram Willits, but then Postmaster of Willitsville (Willits today) was on the stage. The robbery took place near Robber's Rock about five and a half miles from Willits, Supposedly Bart again only realized about $300.00. So much for the mythology that Bart lived for months on end in upscale lodging houses in San Francisco.

Laban Harding Gruwell lived in the same town as Alvy Boles when Boles was nearly beaten to death in 1872. And "Labe's" family tradition holds that while driving a stage south out of Lower Lake, CA, "Labe" was held up and robbed by the famous California outlaw, Black Bart. I could find no proof. But records show that "Labe" owned a livery stable and stage coach line in Lake Co. and had just become a County Supervisor in 1881

Robbery No. 24

Just a month later Bart was again trying for better luck and he hit the La Porte to Oroville stage just five miles out of La Porte July 13, 1882 and it was loaded with gold. But Hackett, the driver, was armed and Bart fled Hackett's fire, lost his derby and supposedly was tracked by dogs. He was by-passed by the detectives, turned off by the skunk odor coming from the hollow log in which Bart was hiding. This log story sequence is amazingly similar to one told by Joaquin Miller about someone being trapped in a log by a mother bear.

Robbery No. 25

Bart, our Alvy Boles-as we know him- having had such a run of bad luck he evidently returned to Shasta Co. and the miners and Indians that he knew. Perhaps he was again staying at Brock's cabin on the Pit River for his next robbery was a repeat. Again it was the same stage, place and driver as his Oct. 8, 1881 robbery but this time he gets only a few dollars on his Sept. 17. 1882 repeat.

It was his last robbery of an Oregon Coast Overland Stage Coach, Horace Williams was the driver and it was the same place on Bass Hill. His take was reputedly only35 cents.

Robbery No. 26

Bart finished off 1882 with a robbery November 23 in Sonoma, Co. at Geyser Rd. of the Lakeport to Cloverdale stage just about five miles out of Cloverdale. Bart actually got $457.50 this time. And Collins and Levene's 1992 quotation of a letter written from an Aull to a Brastow in Calistoga must be quoted in part here as it had relevance in ways they could not have been aware.

"Dear Sir, I wrote you on yesterday from Cloverdale, came through to this place last night via the Geysers. The stage robber was tracked along top of Ridge 15 near the Geysers, he came to scene of robbery and went the same route. I found on arrival here that "Buck" English was discharged last month from San Quentin. "Buck" has served two terms from Lake Co., once for robbery, last term 8 years. During the last term he was the inseparable companion of Jack Bowen (Black Jack), Big Frank Clark, Billy Miner, et. al. He fills the modern rendition of the Jeffersonian test, "He is capable, he is 'on it." He lives at Middletown, Lake Co., 18 miles north of this place, and on direct line of route the stage robber went and came from scene of robbery. While all the ear marks are those of Black Bart, still "Buck" is bright enough to ape his style if he knew it. I go to Middletown and Lower Lake on stage today."

Collins and Levene opined: **Perhaps English was guilty, but no evidence was found to charge him.**

Buck English didn't get out of jail until 1882. And what Levene, Hume and the rest didn't know was that both Joaquin Miller and

Alvy Boles had known various good and bad members of the English family in their Shasta, Siskiyou, and Idaho days.

It was Harry L. Wells who wrote in his book (Wells 1881, p.119) that among a band of notorious outlaws who had lived on an island in Scott Valley were Frank Tompkins, Nels Scott, and Jack Marshall whom Wells suggested had actually sprung Miller from jail in Shasta in 1859.

Probably so, but the 1860 census puts Nelson Scott age 25 with other Scotts getting their mail at Callahan in South Siskiyou Co. Jack Marshall who had arrived at the age of 13 or so, in 1825 from Liverpool England on the ship *John Wells*. Was in the 1860 U.S. Census listed as living at Humbug, Siskiyou Co., not far from the Boles mine.

By now we all realize how well Miller and Boles knew so many men in Scott Valley and so would still know them all in the later days of the Idaho gold rush. So it would have been perfectly normal for Black Bart, aka. Alvy Boles, to have visited a few days with any family named English living near Middletown, Lake Co., CA.

Miller sometimes wrote of some of the bad men he too had known... "Why there was Red Hat hanged at Deer Lodge [MT]; Locklash [Lockhart] killed at Pit River [by CA Indians]; Sam Locklash [Harry Lockhart's twin] killed at Orophee [Oro Fino City] two miles south of Pierce City]; Cherokee Bob killed at Millersburgh, [OR]; Nels Scott; Dave English hanged at Lewiston [ID]—and so on, and so on,"

And only 20 or so miles away down from where English lived there lived in Pope Valley in Sonoma Co. John Bird Markham, brother of Edward A. Markham who gave us the afore-mentioned poem "Mendocino Memory". And who identified Black Bart, after his capture, as the man who had offered him a job when he met him while herding sheep on a trail in Mendocino Co. John Bird

Markham would have been 21 in 1852 Oregon City, OR when Joaquin Miller with his parents arrived there, and the families became acquainted. Mrs. Markham and Mrs. Miller became lifelong pen pals and promoters of their sons' literary interests. Both women later died in Oakland, Alameda Co. CA.

John and Edward's father was Samuel Barzillai Markham, b. 1792 in Vermont and d. abt. 1878 in Oregon City, Clackamas Co. OR, but was buried in a Millersburg, OR cemetery. Samuel, like other Oregonians tried his hand at gold mining in California but was unsuccessful and returned to farming in Oregon. It would be difficult to presume that Samuel Markham who had been in Ohio and had captained a wagon train to Oregon in 1847 didn't know Alvy Boles in his Yreka days. And his son John Bird Markham died in 1912 on the Harrison Gulch property where he and his family had mined for years. And by which property passed the road from Milleville in Shasta Co. to the Mendocino Coast. Harrison Gulch was named for Judge W.R. Harrison who had freed Alvy Boles in the 1850's when Alvy Boles was accused of murder.

Thus the road from Brock's place on the Pit River through Milleville to Mendocino Co. passed through Harrison Gulch in Shasta Co. CA.

Robbery No.27

Bart began his eighth year robbery circuit April 12, 1883 with yet another hit on the Lakeport to Cloverdale run at practically the same milepost as before and he gained only $32.60. Again they tracked him east to the Geysers area in Sonoma Co.

It was Nov. 24, 1883 and Black Bart was back in Sonoma Co. and robbed the stage from Lakeport to Cloverdale on that famous "longest 30 miles in the World." It was his 26th robbery and he was back among friends. The Asbill place was not far off and Asbills had kin in Bodega, Sonoma Co. Also then living in Bodega [from 1864-1884] lived J.S. [L?] Cummings. He was formerly in Yreka 1852-57 and a founder of the Masons there in Yreka. He was living in Bodega in his last days. Was Black Bart just passing through or stopping by to see an old friend? Did Black Bart winter in San Francisco or with relatives elsewhere? We don't know. But he was back in Sonoma Co. for a repeat robbery on April 12, 1883 of the stage from Lakeport to Cloverdale just as he had done on Nov. 24, 1882.

Of this last robbery in the coastal area Frank Asbill wrote from what he had heard:

"At this point [where Bart had discarded his gun] they took up Bart's trail. It led east over the San Hedren Mountain, and continued straight on toward the Sacramento Valley. The distance over the high mountain to the west side of the Sacramento Valley being about 150 miles, as the crow flies. The trip took [sheriff] Montgomery two nights and one day.

He used three horses and never stopped to rest. Black Bart went a foot. When Montgomery got to Arbuckle, a small town on the west side of the Sacramento Valley he learned that Black Bart had lost no time. He had taken a train from Arbuckle only an hour before Montgomery got there. Montgomery traced Black Bart over the Sierra Nevada Mountains into Nevada. That was the last ever heard of the noted bandit Black Bart – Mr. Charles Bolton." (*The Last of the Far West* p.165).

Robbery No.28

Perhaps Bart wintered in Nevada but on June 23. 1883 Black Bart committed his 28th robbery in nearby Amador Co. CA. This time it was the stage from Jackson to Ione. He may have even stayed on in those foothills to be with family. For Nov.1(17?) 1883 Alvy Boles became a grandfather to Carrie (Caroline) Boles born in Placerville, El Dorado Co. CA, where his son Emery Allison Boles (born 1841 in Brimfield., Portage Co., OH) was then living (DB).

Collins and Levene wrote that mail and packages were staged to Jackson from there gathered together and staged on to Ione. And just four miles out of Jackson as the stage pulled up to the top of the Morrow Grade, true to form, Bart pulled off his robbery. Bart's loot totaled $750.00. Collins and Levene labeled it "A last hurrah! "And as usual trackers lost Bart as usual...

Chapter 23

Bart's Last Robbery

Only two days later, Nov. 6, 1883, Black Bart committed his 29th robbery. It was the stage from Sonora to Milton in nearby Calaveras Co. and it became his last

Chapter 24

Capture

Bruce Levene wrote in detail in 1992 all about Bart's capture November 7-13, 1883 in San Francisco and the detectives and others involved. But Black Bart never did reveal his true identity and Levene in 1992 was still under the impression that Black Bart was C. E. Boles from New York so Levene compared Bart's history to that of the detectives from the same area.

Actually Detective Hume had been in law enforcement in and around Placerville, CA during some of the later robbery years when Black Bart would have been visiting there his son Emery Allison Boles who was a Mason and lived next to the cemetery where Boles were buried. And Detective Thorn had been a Sheriff in Calaveras Co.

Another difficulty with the capture story is the two pages torn from C. E. Bole's bible and folded into the bible in Alvy Boles possession. We may never know where in Alvy's mining travels he met up with the real C. E. Boles, or how he may have obtained those pages that he allowed them to identify him by. But we do know C.E. Boles never returned home.

Yet another recent book on Black Bart "The Search is Over" by Robert Jernigan & Wiley Joiner is about C.E. Bolton as Black Bart. Took its inspiration from "The Poet Bandit" by Gail Jenner and Lou

Legerton who list in their acknowledgements Bob Jernigan. Both books followed Joaquin Millers use of the name Charles Bolton in his "What Bart Says" in The Examiner after the release of Boles/Bolton. When Miller was protecting his friend Alva Boles and offered him a chance to stay at his Oakland Heights, just as Miller had protected Chris Evans, the train robber. He also helped Evans publish.

Remember Joaquin Millers cousin John Miller was California's first senator, followed by George Hearst who also lived on the McCloud River.

O'Reilly's recent *Legends & Lies* doesn't even know of Alvy Boles. They just used the lies and misdirection's of journalists, the easy research such as loose pages in a bible. As for Bart's Bolton alias, he may have just borrowed it from a Bolton he had met in San Francisco.

Newspaper articles tell us that Bart was...Taken to the Central Police Station, his name was placed on the 'small book,' a secret register for prisoners whose cases were under investigation, not ready for public knowledge. However, the *Call*'s beat reporter speculated that someone booked as 'Fleming' back at the City Prison might actually be Black Bart. When the desk sergeant asked his name, Bart replied 'T. Z. Spaulding,' adding another alias to his list. Perhaps the Call reporter mixed up Fleming with Spaulding, or perhaps Hume provided the 'Fleming' name to further confound the ever-inquisitive press.

Chapter 25
Confession/Confusion

Arrest accounts vary in the name given Black Bart, C.E. Bolton, Bart, C.E. Boles and Spaulding were among those names used, and gave rise to some of the present day spurious stories about who Black Bart really was. Accounts differ as to method of travel, names given, and myths continue to abound.

And Hume's self serving reports on the robberies continue in the *San Francisco Call*. Various stories appeared that told differing versions of Humes self serving story purported to be confession. Which add nothing to our knowledge.

When Bart was threatened with life in prison for his crime he asked to make a deal. If he would show them the money for the last robbery then he would only go to prison for a short time. Several theories have surfaced about the confession to all the robberies, such as; simply getting his sentence reduced by helping them "close" unsolved robberies; afraid of the Postal Department as one of the robberies had rifles through mail, and he didn't want to face charges from the U.S. Government According to all accounts, on the following Tuesday morning Bart walked into a Sacramento barber shop for a shave and haircut. Then from one of the town's better tailors, ordered a suit of clothes. That afternoon he left for Reno on the eastbound train.

He spent the next two or three days in Reno, or as we now know, more likely in Genoa, NV. While in Nevada, he wrote the owner of the Webb House, at 37 Second Street in San Francisco, to say that he would be back in the city shortly. (*Black Bart, Boulevardier Bandit* pg.71 and Wells Fargo 1883 S.F Directory). Then on Nov. 9, Hoeper has Black Bart back on the train to Sacramento to pick up his new suit. Then Bart returns to San Francisco for one night's stay in an unknown hotel before checking in at the Webb House. [Curiously Hoeper then gives the address as 27 Post Street]. The Webb House was near the Palace Hotel and the centers of commerce and publishing in those days.

While in Nevada Black Bart may not have stayed in Reno but would have visited either his son A.B.'s farm in Douglas Valley or even more likely his son Emery Allison Boles the blacksmith and wagon maker in Genoa, NV.. And E.A. seemed to have been living in both Genoa and Placerville, El Dorado Co. CA, where we find him registered to vote in 1884 as Emery Allison Boles (b.1841/42). Remember! E.A. Boles was in Placerville and a Mason at the same time as was Edward Markham.

And as for the Confession, Black Bart had only confessed to the robberies and allowed himself to be identified as C. E. Boles and/or Charles Bolton or whatever they wanted to call him. He hadn't volunteered who he really was or his real age.

Chapter 26

Recognition

When Black Bart (aka Alvy Boles) was arrested he was held in the San Francisco City Prison before being returned and tried in Placerville, El Dorado Co. And possibly again in San Fransisco, before being sent on to San Quentin. Among the curious viewing him there in San Francisco was the aforementioned Beard Wooster, then working as a bookkeeper at the Palace Hotel. Who had formerly had worked at the Reader Ranch and who wrote them identifying Black Bart as "Mr. Martin." (Greg Watkins 1993).

Perhaps Beard Wooster really only saw one of the many photo cards floating around. Collins and Levene also quote (p. 224-225) from Joaquin Miller's friend Gertrude Atherton's book *My San Francisco* (ca. 1940) how Alexander Robertson, a clerk at C. Beach's Montgomery St. bookstore, had been shocked on finally seeing Black Bart's picture in the paper to realize that he knew him as Mr. Samson, "a mild mannered dark man with an excellent literary taste and fascinating personality."

Long after Bart's picture was in the papers my old friend Helen Hogue asked George Albro, then custodian of the Shasta County Jail, if ever he had seen the notorious Black Bart. Albro responded: "I believe I have seen him many times and talked with him….A man answering his description would be around the livery stable and hotel in Shasta. He posed as a miner and I believe it was Black Bart, or Charles E. Boles as he really was." Note, Albro started work as a youngster in Shasta and probably never knew Boles' real name or like all other locals chose to not remember it.

But historian Helen Hogue's Albro story was bested by May Hazel Southern, first President of the Shasta Historical Society. She had lived at her father's stage stop/hotel called "Sims" on the Sacramento River. She too recognized the real Alvy Boles from his picture and recalled robbery 10 Oct. 25, 1879 when Mrs. Bigelow from Butteville (Edgewood today) was a passenger on the stage and Bart had had her sit up front with the driver so he could keep an eye on her. It was written that this robbery occurred ten miles north of Redding on Bass Hill and James Smithson was the driver. This was his last trip as he had just purchased Charles's Station at Slate Creek. There he would probably see many times during the next few years the person [Alvy Boles] whom Black Bart really was.

Had it not been so dark and had she not been so frightened Mrs. Bigelow might have recognized something about her sometimes neighbor." For he had often been through Butteville[Edgewood] since first growing vegetables there in 1853, then having a saw-mill there until moving it to the Fall River area in 1856. And he was still doing itinerant blacksmithing in the area in 1879. Ralph Bigelow, his wife Emily, and their children lived in Edgewood, [Butteville] in Shasta Valley, Siskiyou Co. from at least 1860 onward. Note that in Southern's 1948 manuscript she still did not reveal Bart's true name. (Southern 1948 #2 p. 97).

Another person who saw Bart's picture related to May Hazel Southern his own encounter with Black Bart. It seems that when Bart was in Redding, Bart stayed at the City Hotel on Market St. near Tehama St. A Mr. N.J. Pehrson was the proprietor and bar keeper. He said that one dark and rainy night a stranger sat late reading in the bar room. Mr. Pehrson didn't want to count the money into the till in front of a stranger so he slipped it into a large belt he wore and slapped on a revolver under his coat. He told the stranger, "It is 2 A.M. and I am closing." The stranger replied. "It is not safe for you to go alone. I will escort you." Mr. Pehrson wasn't robbed or killed and he forgot the incident until later when he saw Bart's picture in the paper after his capture.

Chapter 27

San Quentin

On Nov. 21, 1883 records show Black Bart was admitted to San Quentin as:

> "C.E. Bolton, Charles Bolton # 11046]. origin New York, for Robbing, term of sentence 6 years, age 48 [sic], included in identifying marks; height 5' 7" blue eyes, gray hair, two missing front teeth [see 1872], and two missing lower teeth (California State Archives)."

[Note: Gray hair at 48? There was a Bolton from New York and there were Boles who had also come from New York.]

The Pundits Report.

Only a few weeks later on Dec. 16, 1883 in the S.F. *Morning Call* came the story about the "Lost Cabin Mine" written by an (H.L.W.). Who was H.L.W.?

I originally thought it was Harr L Wagner, then Miller's manager, but I was mistaken. It was Harry L Wells whose book *History of Siskiyou County 1881* had just been on the market for a couple years.

Yes, you remember correctly. Harry L. Wells had already published this "Lost Cabin" story in his *History of Siskiyou County,*

California 1881 wherein he had bemoaned Miller's earlier telling about the same story in his 1873 *Life Amongst the Modocs.*

In 1881 Wells wrote about Joaquin "No one expects a poet to tell the truth, even when he makes a pretense of doing so." Wells had been editor of *West Shore* in Portland, OR since the spring of 1883. It seemed Miller had reworked his article for the *Call* to read as if while interviewing Black Bart at San Quentin, he learned the Lost Cabin story, which he had actually already written about way back in 1871.

What were Wells' reasons for not identifying Alvy Boles as Black Bart? Was he grateful for the help that Boles had been to him in his Siskiyou research or was he fearful it would be negative publicity for his soon to be published academic style *History of Nevada Co.*, (Oakland, Thompson and West, Rept. Berkeley. Howell North Books, 1990).

Miller's reasons seemed more personal since he had known Alvy Boles as a benefactor from Miller's first days in Yreka in 1854. And perhaps Miller, in 1883, already had some inklings as to Black Bart's real identity. Miller had just written about the "Pit River Massacre" San Francisco *Chronicle* (Mar. 25/83).

Now here was Boles in San Quentin where Ambrose Bierce and Miller would visit him later. Boles hadn't hurt or killed anyone. He was serving his time. And both Wells and Miller were writing for the *Overland Monthly* and the *San Francisco Call*. "The Lost Cabin" story was being repeated by many other papers, like *The Brooklyn Daily Eagle,* Sunday, Jan. 27 1884. See the Appendix for the whole story of how the gold mine that was guarded by a grizzly was found and how it was lost again.

As for Miller, references to his "Lost Cabin Mine" story go back to 1871 Boston publication of his *Songs of the Sierras.* In a July 27, 1871 review in New York's *Evening Post* p.2, cols. 4, 5 where a copy of a letter appeared from the English critic George Francis Armstrong. Yet another letter, source unidentified, which included the story of the "Lost Cabin Mine" as told to the writer by Joaquin Miller in England in 1870/71:

Our Appendix version of the "Lost Cabin Mine" story was written by Wells (Wells 1881, 116 & 117). But in *The San Francisco Morning Call* Sunday, December 16, 1883. Vol. LV (16):1:3, 4.). H.L.W. [Harry L. Wells] published this same story after Bart was put into San Quentin. So it is obvious that Joaquin Miller (1871) and Harry L. Wells had both obtained their "Lost Cabin" stories from Alvy Boles. So December 16, 1883 publishing is obviously Wells's way of outing the jailed C.E. Boles, or Bolton, as Alvy Boles, from whom they had both received the "Lost Cabin Mine" story.

Some will still argue that despite all the evidence that Alvy Boles, aka. Black Bart, was in jail in 1884, records say Alvy Boles age 71 b. OH, was a Blacksmith, in Yreka, CA.While Alvy Boles was, on Sept. 6, registered to vote and this registration was carried forward to 1886. Is this just a clerical error? Remember they said he was dead in the massacre. But there is no evidence that he voted during those years or any mention of any other activity for him, obvioiusly in jail. He was not in the 1884 Siskiyou Co. Great Register. Records of who actually voted seem to no longer exist, if they ever did. And beware of undocumented on-line later day accounts that still have Alvy Boles in 1885 as a Blacksmith, on Yreka Creek in Yreka CA.

Even before, and while, Alvy Boles was in San Quentin many of his friends and relatives had moved about. The Cummings of Alvy's early Yreka days had moved from Bodega to Dry Creek in Sonoma Co. Alvy's son A.B. was still in Douglas Co. Nevada, E.A. Boles seemed to be both in Genoa, NV and Placerville, CA.

Joaquin Miller's friends had moved about too. He had heard

that his Shasta/Siskiyou friend Amanda, his acknowledged *Wintu* woman, who had been living at the little Sacramento River Bridge, where the Pit River joined the Sacramento, was then working at Sisson's fishing resort over on the McCloud River. This place, an ancient Indian crossing became part of the Hearst estate.

While over in London, Lotta Crabtree, Yreka's "Little Lotta" of the winter of 1855/56, had become a theatrical star. She supposedly was worth five to six million dollars when she retired from the stage in 1891.

Joaquin Miller was again back in the States in New Orleans writing on the South and enjoying the hospitality of George Washington Cable [1844-1925], a native-born columnist/reporter for the *New Orleans Picayune* and friend of Miller's friend Samuel Clemens (Mark Twain).

From Cable's house Miller wrote: "The Opening of the World's Fair at New Orleans" for New York's *The Independent* (Jan.1/85), "New Orleans and the World's Exposition" for *The Times*. Chicago (Jan. 4/56), "In the Land of Ponce de Leon" for *The Independent* (Feb. 5/85), and lastly "Sunday at Fort Sumter." For *The Independent* (Apr.16/85), a description of Charleston and the surrounding area.

As usual, Miller was carrying on his correspondence with Charles Warren Stoddard. His Feb. 7, and Mar. 2 letters to him were on St. Charles Hotel, New Orleans stationery.

Mrs. Frank Leslie had arrived in February with her friend Mrs. Pierce, and her advertising manager, Herbert Bridgman, to inspect the Cotton Centennial Exposition and enjoy a carnival ball.

They stayed at the St. Charles hotel. Mrs. Leslie had called on her contributor Ella Wheeler Wilcox, but Mrs. Leslie breakfasted with Miller at Cable's house. She had no ticket to the ball and none could be arranged for her but at midnight she showed up in her diamonds etc., and Miller took her to the ball of the Knights of

Momus at the French Opera House. There they led the grand march at the opening of the New Orleans Exposition, hence his article "The Three Merry Days of New Orleans [sic]." in *The Independent* (Mar. 5/85).

Miller wrote: "This fabulous woman had come from New York to New Orleans, attended the exposition, reigned queen of the carnival ball and was back to her desk at work, in less than a week. I know of no one in history so remarkable, so glorious as this strangely beautiful, and inspired little Creole. She was said to have been making an annual profit of $100,000 from her publications containing the latest of Ella Wheeler Wilcox's and"...Miller's work. Of course this publisher and Miller were rumored to be more than close friends. And later when she was widowed and came to San Francisco he invited her to stay at the "Hights," but when she saw the place, she fled back to her posh San Francisco hotel where she had arranged for rooms spacious enough that her maid could sleep in the parlour.

While Boles was in San Quentin, life for others went on as before. His son, E. A. Boles, and wife C. Boles, lost three children in the 1886 smallpox epidemic. [Grave in Placerville, CA.]

Various accounts have Boles being visited by a Civil War surgeon Dr. J.H. Hostettler. (Collins and Levene ibid. p.184) Actually Boles was visited, according to Joaquin Miller, by Dr. F. C. Horsley who, back in 1859 when Miller was leaving Siskiyou Co., was succeeding Fair as sheriff. (Wells 1881) Still later in the 1870's Horsley had a pharmacy in Canyon City, OR when Joaquin Miller was practicing law there under his own name, C. H. Miller.

In 1886 Harry L. Wells was again repeating his "The Lost Cabin Mine" in *The West Shore* Vol. 12 p. 279-284 [prob. 1886]. Wells had been back in Oregon and was the Editor of *West Shore* from 1883 onward. In this piece he refers to Alvy Boles as living in

Shasta Valley, which he was in 1856. And listed as an itinerant blacksmith, which he was, and as a Kentuckian, when according to all records, Alvy was actually born in Ohio.

McClintock was listed at Bogus in 1877 as a farmer b. 1837 in MA. (GSSC Jennifer Bryan). In 1886 William King McClintock was still listed at Bogus, Siskiyou Co. CA but as a Dairyman not as a farmer. And Bogus on the Klamath was only 21 miles from Yreka and just a few miles from robberies numbers 3, 14, 15, 16, and 17. Remember we already know Alvy was still registered to vote and this registration was carried forward to 1886. But there is no evidence that he voted during those years or any mention of any other activity for him. And we know he hadn't been in the 1884 Siskiyou Co. Great Register. Records of who actually voted seem to no longer exist, if they ever did exist. And beware of undocumented on-line later day accounts that still have Alvy Boles in 1885 as a Blacksmith, on Yreka Creek in Yreka CA. That list was put out by the same newspaper editor that we know had to have known Alvy Boles well, yet who only gave him a paragraph in his paper when he died in 1890.

Please note too; The Great Register for General Election, Nov. 2, 1886 (for Siskiyou Co.) has columns labeled (Vote) [no entries made so a pre-election list only] (Name) (Occupation) and (Last Residence) (Naturalization-Date, Place and by what court). The last column for Alvy Boles, 71 b OH shows Reg. date of Sept 6, 1884, so brought forward from 1884 list and/or possibly before that]. Ancestry. Com. also has 1886 and age 71 that would mean he was born ca. 1815 which is not the date on any census forms. Forms all say 1811/12 in which case he would have been 75 in 1886. So one could assume he was still on the list, although in San Quentin.

Probably, to Alvy Boles, his most important old acquaintance to move in 1886 was Joaquin Miller, who had been living in his poet's cabin in Washington D.C. where he was known also as a successful playwright and sometimes guest at Grover Cleveland's White house. But his term was ending as was Miller's cousin's John Miller, as senator from California. And Miller yearned to return to the site of Frémont's camp overlooking the Bay Area.

Miller soon settled on his "Hights" above Oakland, and resumed his public San Francisco newspaper feud with Ambrose Bierce, while they often drank and sometimes fished together. And it was Bierce who said that "Miller was as great-hearted a man as ever lived." (Phoebe Cutler, "Joaquin Miller and the Social Circle at the Hights." *California* History (*The Journal of the California Historical Society*, Vol. 90, No 1, November 2012, p57.). Both Miller and Bierce worked at times for the Hearst's and visited their ranch in Mexico, near where Bierce later disappeared from sight forever.

Not long after Black Bart was imprisoned at San Quentin Miller wrote the warden asking to interview Black Bart. Miller's name was known not only because of his poetry and journalism but because his cousin John F. Miller was the Senator from California 1881-1886 and was succeeded soon thereafter by Miller's mining and publication friend George Hearst. Consequently Miller and Ambrose Bierce soon spent a night at San Quentin and Bierce immortalized the experience in the following poem which was later published (Joaquin Miller was one of the publishers) in his *Black Beetles in Amber* in 1892:

THE CONVICTS' BALL

San Quentin was brilliant. Within the halls
Of the noble pile with the frowning walls
(God knows they've enough to make them frown,
With a Governor trying to break them down!)

Was a blaze of light. 'Twas the natal day
Of his nibs the popular John S. Gray.
"The ball is free!" cried Black Bart, and they all
Said a ball with no chain was a novel ball;
"And I never have seed," said Jimmy Hope,
"Such a lightsome dance withouten a rope."
Chinamen, Indians, Portuguese, Blacks,
Russians, Italians, Kanucks and Kanaks,
Chilenos, Peruvians, Mexicans—all
Greased with their presence that notable ball.

None were excluded excepting, perhaps,
The Rev. Morrison's churchly chaps,
Whom to prevent a religious debate,
The Warden had banished outside of the gate.
The fiddler, fiddling his hardest the while,
"Called off" in the regular foot-hill style:
"Circle to the left!" and "Forward and back!"
And "Helium to port for the scabbard tack!"
(This great virtuoso, it would appear,
Was Mate of the Gatherer many a year.)
"Ally man left!"—to a painful degree
His French was unlike to the French of Paree,
As heard from our countrymen lately abroad,
And his "doe cee doe" was the gem of the fraud.
But what can you hope from a gentleman barred
From circles of culture by dogs in the yard?
'Twas a glorious dance, though, all the same:
The Jardin Mabille in the days of its fame
Never saw legs perform such springs—
The cold-chisel's magic had given them wings.

They footed it featly, those ladies and gents:
Dull care (said Long Moll) had a helly go-hence!

'Twas a very aristocratic affair:
The crime de la crime of the place was there—
The swells and belles of our toughest sets,
And Hubert Howe Bancroft sent his regrets.
[Bancroft was the historian of the day.]

While Alvy Boles (Black Bart) was imprisoned he saw supposed family, and answered letters written to him supposedly by family, sugguesting he would see them when he got out of prison. But he never did, he was just protecting his true family. His family eventually acknowledged his death in 1890 with a one line notification in a Nevada paper using only their initials.

Chapter 28

Bart's Life After Prison

Again **Levene's** research up until 1992 gave us the best report on the events quoting from various newspapers.

According to the Examiner, Bart "was very nervous that morning, as though he was trying not to feel too hopeful lest an unforeseen thunderbolt strike him." At 8a.m. Warden McComb (who had succeeded Shirley) called Bart into his office, congratulated him on his new freedom and expressed the hope that prison time had served as a warning, that henceforth Bart would lead an honest life. Bart wore the same dark suit he had been arrested in four years and two months earlier. His gold-headed cane, his silver watch and gold chain, gold collar and cuff buttons were returned, and he was given $5, the amount presented to all outgoing convicts. Bart arrived at the Ferry Building in San Francisco at 9:30 and held an impromptu press conference. An Examiner reporter first asked him if his imprisonment had seemed long. "Not very long to look back on," he answered, "but it was an awful long time in passing." Avowing that prison had left him a changed man, he thanked the prison officials for their kindness and tried to clear up his domestic situation:" "Since my incarceration I have understood that a great many people were of the opinion that I had taken to the road because of domestic difficulties. Such, I assure you ... is not the case. I have for many years had a faithful wife, who has been true to me at all times and she still clings to me. [Is some irritation detected in the choice of 'clings'?] I have also three daughters, who have now grown to womanhood, who entertain the most tender feelings for me. They have been well brought up, and received all the benefits of a first-class education, and I look forward to a very happy reunion with my family (Chronicle, 12/22/88)."

Well, not exactly. Research has shown that Alvy Boles did have three daughters and three sons. the last of which was born while Alvy was working in the new California gold mines having left his expecting wife possibly under the wing of his or her brother. Census data shows that one of the girls was living later with another family and that his wife had joined up with a recently arrived widower and they were raising their children together. Alvy eventually brought the three sons west. Meantime you can figure out how much he may have contributed to the cost of their education and travel west while all the while listing himself as a widower every time the census taker came around.

"It has also been said that during my criminal work I have been guilty of robbing people outside of the corporation of Wells, Fargo & Co. That I positively deny. I never at any time injured any person outside of the express people, and Wells Fargo & Co. are the only persons living to whom I owe one-quarter of a dollar. I know that the mailbag which was on the stage that I stopped near San Andreas — and of course you are aware that is the only stage robbery with which I have been connected was cut open when found, but I tell you truthfully that I didn't cut it. I never intended to tamper with the mail or to injure private individuals in any respect. The mailbags which were rifled must have been cut open by the stage driver or some of the numerous detectives who were hunting arduously for me.

When the [Wells, Fargo] express is robbed, the shippers are reimbursed as soon as the amount is known; but for the people who entrust their money to the United States mail, there is no redress. Their loss is irrevocable. The Government never repays them or makes the slightest effort to recover the money or discover the offender."

As Bart turned to go, one reporter asked if he intended to write more poetry. With a twinkle in his eye, the waggish tendency still there, Bart responded: "Didn't I tell you that I had abandoned crime of every kind?"

The next day inquiring minds noted in the agate type of the Examiners personals column the following cryptic entry:

Black Bart WILL HEAR SOMETHING to his advantage by sending his address to M. R. Box 29, this office.

The ad has never been explained. But you the reader know that George Hearst and William Randolph Hearst were the publishers of *The Examiner*, and you can be sure that Bart was given Millers address, and or other addresses to which he could return. And possibly other financial arrangements could be made.

A week later Examiner columnist Ambrose Bierce celebrated Bart's literary decision, in one stanza of a 40-line poem:

What's that? — you ne'er again will rob a stage?

What! did you so? Faith, I didn't know it.

Was that what threw poor Themis in a rage? I thought you were convicted as a poet.

Obviously Bart wrote to many people while in prison and Mary had been a main correspondent. A letter sent by Bart makes it clear he will not be seeing them soon and he never did. All the C.E. Boles and Bolton story appear to be fabrications,as many an author has penned a book based on this and other correspondence.

And you might also ask, "how come Alvy had C.E. Boles's bible?"

True, Bart had a bible with pages with C.E.Boles wife's inscription to C.E, on two pages torn out and folded in the bible. No one ever proved those two pages came from that bible. Where, when, or how Alvy Boles met C.E. Boles while mining some genealogist or historian may someday be able to tell us. Meanwhile we know that Alvy's ancestors had ties to the N.Y. Boles, way back when, and so maybe they were distant kin. And knowledge of C.E.'s real end might not have been as comforting or profitable as having a "lost husband" turn up as Black Bart the famous stage robber.

Upon Bart's release from San Quentin on Jan. 21 in 1888 Ambrose Bierce wished him well with a poem he wrote in the San Francisco *Examiner* Jan. 29, 1888 and later included in his *Black Beetles in Amber* in1892:

"Black Bart, Po8"

Welcome, good friend; as you have served your term,
And found the joy of crime to be a fiction,
I hope you'll hold your present faith, stand firm
And not again be open to conviction.

Your sins, though scarlet once, are now as wool:
You've made atonement for all past offenses,
And conjugated--'twas an awful pull!--
The verb "to pay" in all its moods and tenses.

You were a dreadful criminal--by Heaven,
I think there never was a man so sinful!
We've all a pinch or two of Satan's leaven,
But you appeared to have an even skinful.

Earth shuddered with aversion at your name;
Rivers fled backward, gravitation scorning;
The sea and sky, from thinking on your shame,
Grew lobster-red at eve and in the morning.

But still red-handed at your horrid trade
You wrought, to reason deaf, and to compassion.
But now with gods and men your peace is made
I beg you to be good and in the fashion.

What's that?--you "ne'er again will rob a stage"?
What! did you do so? Faith, I didn't know it.
Was that what threw poor Themis in a rage?
I thought you were convicted as a poet!

I own it was a comfort to my soul,
And soothed it better than the deepest curses,
To think they'd got one poet in a hole
Where, though he wrote, he could not print, his verses.

I thought that Welcker, Plunkett, Brooks, and all
The ghastly crew who always are begriming
With villain couplets every page and wall,
Might be arrested and "run in" for rhyming.

And then Parnassus would be left to me,
And Pegasus should bear me up it gaily,
Nor down a steep place run into the sea,
As now he must be tempted to do daily.

Well, grab the lyre-strings, hearties, and begin:
Bawl your harsh souls all out upon the gravel.
I must endure you, for you'll never sin
By robbing coaches, until dead men travel.

The public's reaction seems possibly to have been as stated by George Hoeper: "Wells Fargo was not always regarded with deep affection by the general public. In some quarters Wells Fargo's charges were regarded as exorbitant taxes by a ruthless business monopoly. Also, the company's rewards to those who aided it in times of robbery were regarded as 'pinch-penny'. Consequently, the activities of bandits such as Black Bart were tolerated by too many otherwise honest Mother lode citizens. Many looked upon these affairs simply as instances of one thief robbing another. Throughout California and the portions Oregon and Nevada served by Wells Fargo, many were critical of what they considered niggling $100 rewards handed out by the company to citizens and even to its own employees who assisted in thwarting robberies or providing information that brought about arrests of bandits." (*Black Bart, Boulevardier Bandit* 1995 pg.25-6)

Miller's main interest at that time was in his newspaper work, as a newspaper reporter. The Sontag and Evans fight against the railroads was going on and also his friend Black Bart had been reported as last seen in Visalia, the rendezvous point for reporters working the railroad robbery story. Petey Bigelow was covering that for the paper but Miller was sent to do some investigating too. But no story seems to have been signed by Miller. However, Miller became quite involved with the Evans family, even taking them into his home after Evans' capture and their financial destitution.

But later Miller's "The San Joaquin Valley" in Muir's collection had documented his experience with well drilling and land development in the Visalia and Pixley areas for Miller's poet's ear was attuned to the whole business of developing artesian wells in ancient lands and near Pixley where his own dollars had been highly involved. Eventually Miller would set it all down in a poem for children, *Artesia of Tulare* published in *St. Nicholas* (Mar. 1892, No. 19 p.386-70).

Friends with whom Miller corresponded that year included: "My dear Burbank" from San Diego, (Jan.19), Edmund Clarence Stedman, (Feb. 4), Julia Ward Howe, (Jun. 3), "My dear, dear S.... (Oct. 3) 1888 about procuring some lilies for his ponds on his "Hights," several letters to Edwin Bliss Hill and lastly to Edward Markham from "The Heights," December 8, 1888. Note others had influenced Miller's spelling and his daughter Juanita was correcting his spelling.

1888 for Joaquin Miller had been a year full of life. Among his visitors in late summer was Baroness Alexandra Gripenberg of Finland who, while on her literary tour of America, also visited Thomas Wentworth Higginson, Frederick Douglas, Charles Dudley Warner, Mark Twain and Harriet Beecher Stowe. Hugh Hume had suggested the Baroness should see Miller and a meeting was arranged for August 13 at Snell Seminary. The Baroness had just founded the first official women's rights organization in Finland, the Suomen Naisyhdistys (Finnish Women's Association), in Helsinki in 1884. Miller was known not only as a poet/journalist but as a frequent lecturer at teachers association and other feminist meetings in the Pacific West. The Baroness and Miller talked and toured Oakland in his buggy and he entreated her to overnight at his "Hights," to no avail.

Chapter 29

What Bart Says

While spending hours in libraries researching old news-papers for formerly overlooked or unidentified articles for my –now on the internet- "Joaquin Miller Bibliography" I chanced upon, "What Bart Says." *The Daily Examiner,* San Francisco, Sunday, Dec. 2. 1888.

I recognized Miller's writing style and I knew descendants of the people mentioned and I was living on Matquaw Mt. overlooking places described in the article. Thus began my 43 years of research on Black Bart which you have just read.

Collins and Levene included "What Bart Says" in their 1992 *Black Bart* book in their Appendix IV they labeled it "fake and rife with errors." Also in their Appendix *III* titled "Spurious Stories" they labeled Frank Asbill's *The Last of the West* as a "better story than many Black Bart inventions.", But Asbill's story is correct.

And until today Miller's most interesting piece under an alias has never been credited to him. After all, "What Bart Says." *The Daily Examiner,* San Francisco, Sunday, Dec. 2. 1888 was signed "Martin."

Detective Hume and others had been keeping on pinning other robberies on Bart even after his release from San Quentin so William Randolph Hearst chose one of his now so-called "yellow journalists," Joaquin Miller, to set the record straight and to sell a lot of papers.

W.R. Hearst and Joaquin Miller were more than just newspaper owner and reporter. W.R.'s father George Hearst was appointed and later elected the Senator from California upon the death of Joaquin Miller's cousin California's Senator John F. Miller. And it was W.R.'s mother Phoebe Apperson Hearst and Miller who, through news articles had promoted the establishment of free kindergartens in San Francisco as well as other projects. And it was Phoebe who vacationed in Dunsmuir before George bought land on the McCloud River where all the Indian trails had crossed the McCloud River at Huckleberry Creek which is now known as Hearst's Wyntoon.

So what came about in 1888 was "What Bart Says." *The Daily Examiner*, San Francisco, Sunday, Dec. 2., signed "Martin" [Joaquin Miller using the same pseudonym as Black Bart used when he was working on the Reader Ranch]

Back in 1883 there had been a story by a reporter "H.L.W." [Harry L. Wells] who supposedly visited someone in Siskiyou County about Black Bart who was then in prison. Now here we have Joaquin Miller, as Martin, interviewing the recently released Black Bart on an unnamed ranch reached by trails only Miller could have described. The story "What Bart Says" ended up at the site where Jim Brock and Miller had lived just off the Pit River. Basically verifying that Alva Boles had been the person to give the mining information to Miller.

The writer [Miller] supposedly got off the train at Old Pollock [now Lower Salt Creek, originally in *Wintu: Tubaste –eating while running & puywakat entering from east side creek*] rented a horse, followed up Lower Salt Creek, the same as Miller had when he escaped from Shasta's jail in 1859. Then on over and down Hirz

Creek crossing the McCloud River and bypassing his old friend J.B. Campbell's ranch, just across the McCloud River from my home. He then followed the Campbell Creek Trail east between Minnesota and Town Mts., then swam his horse across Squaw Valley Creek and went down to Brock Creek. Where Miller had lived with James Brock in the 1850's and where Miller was apprehended by Lockhart in 1859. Having lived all that, Miller could have written it all from memory from anywhere.

Remember also that Alvy Boles had given Miller and his "pardner' their first pointer back in 1854/55 in their early Siskiyou days. That too, was when Miller probably first heard or met Jeremiah B. Campbell, who had become well known in Yreka in the Summer 1853, for being one of the group of ten who rode about 120 miles to recover horses stolen by the Indians from the miners. Another member of that group was Zach Gibbs, who had also been a member of the Spring group who had wiped out the village near the confluence of Dairy and Squaw Valley Creeks near where later Miller had built his first cabin. Gibbs also became a member of the first Siskiyou County militia company organized Dec. 6, 1855 in Humbug City.

So you see W.R. Hearst, of *The Examiner*, knew that in Joaquin Miller he had the right man to seek an interview with the recently released Black Bart. But it must have been Miller who chose the name "Martin" for that of the interview as Miller knew that was also the alias Black Bart had used when he worked on the Reader Ranch. And I then, on reading the article in 1978, realized that Joaquin Miller knew The Real Black Bart. So my search really began with Hearst's eye catching headlines Dec. 2, 1888 in *The Daily Examiner:*

What Bart Says

The Ex-Highwayman's Story of His Life and Strange Exploits
Hume is contradicted
in "Examiner" Man's Adventure With the
Road-Agent Poet in the Mountains.
WHY BART TOOK TO THE ROAD
How a Great Detective Made a Reputation.
A ROBBER'S MIDNIGHT RIDE.

Hearst of course whetted his reader's appetites with some fabricated telegrams between his "yellow journalist" and the paper:

November 30, 1888

To the Managing Editor Examiner, San Francisco:

I spoke. Have seen the man of whom Am under absolute obligation to conceal where abouts. Will send interview if you guarantee strict compliance with conditions. As wires may leak, will forward under cover to--------by Wells-Fargo. Martin

SAN FRANCISCO, November 30

T0 __ ___, __: Guarantee given. Send story as soon as possible. Hire courier to catch train at _____ if necessary. Don't spare expense to save time.

W.R. Hearst

The above telegrams passed between the editor of the Examiner and a special correspondent at a point which, for reasons that will appear, cannot be named. The correspondent had declared his belief that by going to a certain place named he could get information about Black Bart, who, the detectives say, has been robbing Wells, Fargo &Co.'s stages with his customary diligence and skill in the northern part of the State. He was not at liberty to say upon what he founded that belief, and in response to the suggestion that he might find it somewhat embarrassing to interview a gentleman who carried a shotgun and would have particular objections to being found, he replied that he did not believe Bart had taken to the road again, and as he was not going in search of him in the role of a detective, he was ready to take all the chances.

The telegram at the head of the column was the next that was heard of the correspondent, and it indicates the result of his trip. Following is his detailed account of the affair:

IN SEARCH OF BLACK BART

The particulars of my journey to where I now am cannot be given because it would be impossible even to describe the route or the character of the roads without giving "clewe"s which I am bound to withhold. Therefore I am somewhat hampered in my work and obliged to omit certain facts which ought otherwise to be stated. By accident the whole affair assumed a personal phase, which seems to make it almost necessary to tell the story in the first person. However, you can change that if your editorial judgement so dictates. [The above was a note to the editor, but is published because it serves to introduce the correspondent's account without betraying confidence, and also explains the abruptness of the beginning of the narrative.]

After leaving the railroad, on my journey for the Examiner in search of information concerning the man who Wells, Fargo & Co.'s detectives accuse of having robbed the stages frequently, I went to a ranch about two miles from the station and bought a horse, saddle and bridle and pushed on toward _____'s mountain ranch, where I expected to get reliable directions or possibly meet the man himself. Having known Bolton when he was a mining man, I hoped to be able to recognize him unless he had made very radical changes in his appearance. [Note: Miller was still protecting Alvy Boles by using one of the names (Bolton) by which Black Bart had been arrested]

It was at least twenty-five miles to the ranch, and night came on before I had made half the distance. To make things still more uncomfortable, it began to rain copiously, and of course I was drenched to the skin.

I might have stopped at a house near the creek about half way, but thought it best not to lose any time, and, besides, I would have to lie furiously to ward off the questions that certainly would be asked a man applying for lodging in that part of the country at that time of night. To avoid country curiosity and to lose no chance of finding what I was after, I urged the horse on through the rain and mud, and when I struck the steep mountain trails I found that my animal was no good. He was all knocked-up forward, wheezed like an exhaust pipe and kept me in constant fear of being pitched over his worthless head and breaking my own valuable neck.

AN ADVENTURE IN THE MOUNTAINS

It was somewhere near 9 o'clock P.M. when I heard the sounds of a horse's hoofs on the road ahead of me, and as the sounds came no nearer it was clear that somebody was traveling the same road and in the same direction. A little urging hastened the pace of my horse, and going down a steep place toward a stream I made out the figures of a horse and rider about half way across the ford. I hailed the man, and when he answered the hail I told him that I didn't know the ford very well and wished he would hold on and pilot me across

"All right," he replied, "the rain has swollen the stream some and you'll have to be careful. Got a good horse?"

"No, he isn't worth a cuss. All bunged up."

"Well, I'll wait for you, stranger, right here. Come in a little above that rock and point straight for me."

Following his directions I rode into the stream and the horse picked his way with some trembling among the loose, rolling stones on the bottom. The water was breast high in the middle, where the stranger was, and just as I ranged up alongside and noticed that he was watching me narrowly, my fool of a horse stumbled, twisted his foreleg between two stones and went down. I fell out of the saddle on the side next to the stranger, and reaching for something instinctively I caught his stirrup. My horse was down stream from his, and rolling over in the water, was swept down by the swift current and lost to sight in a moment.

The stranger's tall, strong horse stood braced against the current, and when the man stooped and grasped my coat-collar he spoke sharply to the animal and in another moment we were in shallow water. As the rain had drenched me already, the dunking made no appreciable addition to my discomfort, but I had lost a horse, saddle and bridle for the Examiner, and had a five-mile tramp ahead of me.

I began to thank the man for his help, but he interrupted me with: "Don't mention it. That's a bad place at night, even if he wasn't worth a cuss. But, then, you might have broken your neck if you kept him, so perhaps you've got something to be thankful for. Where are you going?"

"I'm trying to get to_____'s place."

"H'm! Know anybody up there?"

"Yes, I've been acquainted with _____for some years. My name is _____ _____. I'm from San Francisco."

The man told me to get up behind him, as he was going to the ranch, and as he leaned over to give me a hand, I thought I recognized the contour of his face, but I said nothing. When I was seated, and we had got along a hundred yards, said abruptly:

"Still in the newspaper business?"

I replied that I was, and after a pause he said:

"I don't want to be inquisitive, but what do you expect to find at _____'s ranch that will be interesting to newspaper readers?"

"You."

"Well, I'll be there pretty soon."

There was nothing more to be said, but a good deal to be thought, and so we rode along in silence through the rain until we arrived at the ranch. There was a light in the window, and when we rode up to the house the owner of the place came to the door to meet us. Naturally, he was surprised at seeing me, but did not appear in the least disturbed. I was careful not to make any break in the matter of names and did not attempt to explain anything until I heard him address my companion as "Mr. Watkins" (That was not the name, but it will do.) Then I told the adventure at the ford and said I had come up to see Mr. Watkins about a mining proposition.

After getting into dry clothes and outside of a delectable hot rum punch, we had supper, and then our host showed us our rooms and bade us good night. As "Mr. Watkins" went in at his door he nodded over his shoulder to indicate that he wanted me to follow, and a few minutes later I went into his room. There was a queer, dry smile on his face, but no trace of uneasiness, as he motioned me to sit down. He opened the conversation.

FACE TO FACE

"It is some years since we met," he said, "and I believe the last time I saw you we were in a courtroom. I think you were writing down something for a newspaper," and again he smiled.

"Yes," I replied," that was some time ago, and we were not very well acquainted then. But to-night we have become somewhat acquainted, and I am placed under deep obligation to you, as without your help I might have gone down stream with the poor old plug."

"Oh, it was only a bit of luck that my stirrup was there for you to grab. The rest was nothing. But you said you came up to see me. What can I do for you?"

"Give me an interview for the EXAMINER"

He looked at me intently for a moment, seeming somewhat troubled, and then said: "That's a job I don't very well like. I'm not much of a talker for newspapers, and I don't see what I can tell you that will do anybody any good. To speak plainly, I don't think it exactly a square deal for the papers to keep hammering away at a man after everything is all over. Now, what in the world put [it] into your head to come up here looking for me?"

For reply I handed him the San Francisco papers containing Detective Hume's statements about Black Bart and watched him while he read them. Sometimes he smiled, and more frequently he frowned, and when he finished he said: "A little truth and a pretty strong dose of lie. I can deny a lot of this stuff, if that is what you want, but what's the use? You don't want to print that Black Bart says he isn't robbing stages because everybody would say, 'Of course he'd deny it; he wouldn't be likely to tell a reporter that he'd gone on the road again.' And, besides, how are you going to print anything without letting people know where I am? You can see that I wouldn't like that. Here's Hume swearing that Black Bart is at it again, offering rewards and threatening imprisonment for life."

"I can fix it so that nobody will know where you are, and you can rest assured that there will be no chance of a leak in the EXAMINER office."

"Perhaps, but you forget those very clever detectives. You don't know how smart those detectives are, and you never will know unless you ask them and give them a chance to tell you. No, I don't take kindly to the interview idea. Don't you think you had better drop it and go fishing or something?

"No, I'm fishing for news, and a man can't go back and tell fairy tales about that kind of angling. He must show up his string and have the weight verified by the man with the blue pencil. I've got to have an interview in some shape or go out of the business."

"Mr. Watkins" mused a while, the expression on his face varying with the thoughts passing through his mind, and at last he said: "It's a long trip to make for nothing, and I don't know but what I'd like to have some matters set right. But I've never been interviewed, and don't like to break the record. Now I don't want you to say that Black Bart said this or that. Write it some other way. Say that an intimate friend of his, somebody who knows him better than Mr. Hume does, told you what I am going to tell you."

Very well, I replied, "I will keep your record unbroken technically, and I won't give any "clewe" to your whereabouts, but you must leave the rest to my discretion, tempered by the necessity of making a proper news showing for my journey."

"All right. I suppose I must not hamper you too much. Now, then, Black Bart's friend- you better take notes-his intimate friend, the only man to whom he ever talked much about his life, said: Detective Hume makes a great many mistakes in his pretended 'Life of Black Bart,' some through sheer ignorance and some evidently for motives not wholly credible. He takes pains to abuse C.E. Boles, calling him a pusillanimous wretch, and declaring that there is nothing honorable about him. Let Mr. Hume's opinion be what it may, the fact remains that Black Bart never gained a man's confidence to betray it, never swindled a person in trade, and never plundered working people by taking what they produced, sheltering himself behind laws made to legalize theft. He robbed Wells, Fargo & Co. without pretending that stage robbing was a perfectly legal and commendable occupation. He took the chances of being shot, and at least was frank in his method of obtaining other people's property. I haven't heard him find any fault because he was sent to prison, but I know that what he saw and learned at San Quentin did not fill him with any profound respect for the men who execute the laws or the system which breeds them. All the thieves in San Quentin are not wearing stripes. The biggest robbers are not on the road with shotguns, but they make every man who works stand and deliver."

WHY BART LEFT HIS FAMILY

"But never mind that. Hume says that Boles left his wife and children at a town in Illinois at the close of the war and went to Montana. He didn't. He joined his family in Iowa and tried farming there until he found that it only meant starvation, and then he went west. His wife was a smart, capable woman, who could earn a living by dressmaking. Boles had some education but he had not learned a trade, and his army life did not increase his earning power. The only thing he knew much about was mining, and it was agreed between him and his wife that he should go back to the mines and try to make a stake.

"When he had anything he sent money home. The last time he wrote home before disappearing he sent all the money he had, but it never got there, as he learned from a letter he received shortly afterward from his wife. Then he dis-appeared and he had reasons for his action. He knew that it if he was supposed to be dead, his father, who had property, would look out for his family. Hume describes the family as being 'pinched by poverty and distressed beyond description'. That is not true. Mrs. Boles probably did not put by any money, but she lived comfortably and got along very well.

"When Bart's father died, he left quite a lot of money, and Bart's share went to his wife. It was not a big fortune, but it was enough to assure the family of good living. His wife's name had been Johnson, and she had a brother who also possessed some means. The brother proposed to Mrs. Boles that they should combine their capital, buy a place and live upon and work the farm together, and they did so. While Bart was in prison, Johnson swindled Mrs. Boles out of her property. She was away from the place on a visit, and when she returned she found that her brother had installed a woman in the house and was running things to suit himself. He had taken advantage of her confidence and her ignorance of legal matters to get her property into her own hands, and she found herself practically evicted from her home and robbed of her means."

"Now we come to Hume's statement that Bart wrote a villainous letter to his son-in-law on a flimsy pretext, with the object being of putting an end to correspondence. That is a lie. When Bart learned of his brother-in-law's action he wrote an indignant letter to him. The letter was brief, and in a few words demanded restitution of the property to Mrs. Boles. No doubt, Johnson found it unpleasant reading. Johnson sent the letter back to Warden Shirley, accompanied by a letter from himself, in which he practically admitted what he had done. Johnson wound up with a whining complaint and wanted to know if convicts were allowed to send out abusive letters. Warden Shirley handed the whole correspondence to Bart, not as a rebuke, but for his information."

"But Captain Aull was practically running the prison, and Bart was soon summoned before him. Aull began telling Bart that he would not be allowed to write any more such letters. Bart replied: 'You will not be called upon to pass out any letters for me, but you can't dictate to me what I shall write to anybody I will write what I please. When my letters come to you for approval you can pass judgement upon them, but not otherwise. I believe you are not Warden of this prison' Then Aull put on his official dignity, and said he would not be talked to in that way. 'You have sent for me,' replied Bart,' and opened a conversation. If you don't want to be talked to in my way, you can close the interview by sending me away, but while I am here I will say just what I mean.' That ended the conversation, and Bart sent out any letters he wanted to without regard to Mr. Aull's notions of propriety. Hume evidently got his story about the 'villainous' letter from Aull."

"Now, I can tell you why Hume, Aull and the rest of that crowd are so bitter against Bart. When he first went to prison they were all very friendly. The detectives had been getting a great deal of cheap glory on his account, and he was useful to them.

THAT FAMOUS CONFESSION

"You have heard of Bart's confession, in which he owned up to innumerable stage robberies. Here is the truth about that: After he was convicted Hume had a private talk with him - that is, it was supposed to be private, but probably some-body was within hearing distance. Hume said: 'Now this thing is all over, Bart and nothing you can say can make any difference to you, but you can help me out. I have on my books a long list of robberies that nobody has been arrested for. You can admit to me that you committed them, and I can cross them all off.'"

"Bart declined to do anything of the sort. He said he was not confessing anything.

Hume pleaded with him, saying: 'What difference does it make to you? All I want is to clear up my books and square myself. If you will say that you did them I can make my record clear. Now here's one case; I know you did that."

"Yes, said Bart, 'I did that one, if that is any consolation to you; and as for the rest, you can scratch off whatever you like. I don't care what you do; if you want to clear up your books that is your business.' And that is the substance of the much talked about confession. Hume and the rest of the crowd were very friendly after that. They conceived the great idea of inducing Bart to write a book about himself, giving the history of his life and his exploits. They were to superintend the job, and, of course, they were to be cracked up as the greatest detectives that ever lived. They made the proposition to Bart, and he scornfully rejected it. Then they were not so friendly."

"The detectives and Captain Aull were very anxious to get hold of Bart's diamonds and jewelry, and tried all ways to get them. They came to him with a nice story about his biggest diamond. They said it was a family heirloom, that tender and romantic associations were connected with it, and that the lady to whom it belonged was very anxious to recover it. It was a pretty tale, but it was a lie. Bart happened to know that the diamond had been sent with a lot of others for selection, and was being returned to the diamond merchant when he confiscated it. He wouldn't give it up. And he allowed the schemers to see his contempt for them"

"These great detectives ought to have been satisfied with their rewards. The men really entitled to the money were McConnell, the Copperopolis stage driver, the hunter who helped him, and Harry Morse. McConnell got $100 and the hunter got a beautiful gun, which afterwards burst in his hands. How the rest of the pot was divided, I don't know. It was just an accident that put the "clewe" into the hands of Hume and his associates, and then they had to get Harry Morse to follow it up and catch Black Bart for them."

"Perhaps the queerest fatality was connected with the discovery of Bart's true name. When he first went on the road, he carefully examined all his books and papers and destroyed everything that could reveal his identity, because he did not want his family to know anything about him if he should be caught. When he came to the Bible, which his mother had given to him, he tore out the fly-leaf bearing her name and his, and was about to destroy it, when something impelled him to desist.

He knew it was indiscreet, but he could not tear that fly-leaf up, and so he opened the Bible in the middle and put the sheet between the leaves. But for that, nobody ever would have known him as C.E. Boles, and his family would have been spared a great deal."

HIS FIRST ROBBERY

"Let me tell you how my friend Black Bart came to go upon the road. He was traveling about, looking for something to do, and he spent his last dime. Being hungry, he walked up to a ranch-house where people were eating dinner, determined for the first time in his life to ask hospitality of a stranger. He was not a lazy, dirty tramp, but a traveler out of money and hungry. The owner of the ranch met him at the door and Bart spoke to him, not humbly or beggingly, but man fashion. He said:

'I have walked some distance, and being quite hungry, I would like to have dinner with you. I have no money.' 'Wait here,' said the farmer, as he went inside. Bart took a chair on the porch and waited, and as he sat there two or three dogs came sniffing about him. In a moment the man returned with some scraps of food in a tin dish, and handed the dish to Bart. Bart quietly took the dish and placed it down in front of the dogs."

"Isn't it good enough for you?' asked the farmer. 'No, replied Bart, I do not think such hospitality good enough for anybody.' The farmer said rather surly that he didn't believe in encouraging tramps Bart got up and said: 'This is the first time I ever asked anybody to give me anything, and it will be the last. Hereafter, when I want anything, I shall demand it and take it.'"

"He left the place, and further up the road found another ranch. Nobody was in the house, but through the window he saw food on the table. He went in, ate all he wanted, and left a note, saying that he had taken a dinner, and telling the owner to send his bill if he wanted pay for it, giving his proper address. Of course, he never heard any more of it, and it may be counted as Black Bart's first robbery. After that he demanded what he wanted on the road, and usually he got it. He found stage robbing no trick at all. Why, if he chose, he could go out with no other weapon than an old stick and hold up a stage. George Hackett did take a shot at him once on the Lakeport road, but it was accident that gave him the chance. There were three horses attached to the stage, and Bart stood in front of the leader. This horse was nervous, and jumped around a good deal. Bart took his eyes off the box for a moment and glanced at the horse and, as he did that, the messenger fired. One of the shots struck Bart on the head and knocked him down, partly stunned, but the messenger did not follow up his advantage, and Bart got away."

A MIDNIGHT RIDE AND AN ALIBI

"Here is one case, illustrating his method of working. Never mind where this occurred. Bart went to a country hotel, where the stages stopped at night, and some time before the stage was due he asked the landlord to show him to his room. He told the landlord that he wanted to take the down stage in the morning, and wished to be called early. Then he undressed and got into bed, leaving the candle burning.

Half an hour after the night stage had come and gone he rang for the porter and asked for some water. When the porter had brought the water and gone away Bart got up and dressed, cut an inch off the bottom of the candle to make it appear that it had been burned a long time, and slipped out of the house unobserved. He went down to the river, where he had seen some boats, and paddled across the stream to a field where some horses were staked out. He selected the best horse, made a nose-bridle of the riata, mounted him, swam the stream and followed the stage."

"Knowing the roads and lanes thoroughly, and having a good horse, he got around and ahead of the stage and waited for it at a turn in the road. As the stage approached his horse began to whinny, but he patted the animal's neck and quieted him. The stage came up and was halted, and Bart got what he was after. The stage was driven on, and Bart remounted and rode back at full speed, taking side roads and cutting across open country. He forded the stream again, staked out the horse where the grass was green and thick, paddled back in the boat, slipped into the house and went to bed.

Early in the morning the landlord called him and woke him up."

"When the down stage came along it brought news of the robbery, and Bart joined in the discussion that ensued. Suppose even that one of his cuffs had been found on the road where the robbery occurred. He could have proved by the testimony of the hotel people that he was in bed half an hour after the stage left that night, and the landlord would have sworn that he waked him up in the morning. Mr. Hume may take this as a confession, if he can locate the affair, and perhaps scratch off another unfinished case from his record book."

"Now, I think that is all I can tell you. Where Black Bart has been and what he has done since he left San Quentin is his own business, and you don't want to know anything about it. You can say, however, that he never promised Mr. Hume or anybody else to do or refrain from doing anything whatever. He didn't ask anybody's advice about where he should go; that isn't his way. He is under obligations to none of that crowd, and he cares very little for their abuse. Goodnight."

Historical facts, logic, common sense, and writing styles all lead one to the obvious conclusion that the previous story was not written by the same person who wrote the afore recited version of the "Lost Cabin Story." Only Miller could have written "What Bart Says" carrying the action over the same Indian trails he himself had traversed while fleeing a pursuing posse in 1859.

This so-called interview could have been and probably was conducted at Miller's Oakland "Hights" although Miller later states Black Bart never took him up on his invitation to visit after his release. To me the "give away" was when Miller as "Martin," after having been thoroughly submerged in a stream, could still have readable news clips of Hume's accusations of further robberies, by the just released Black Bart.

The "What Bart Says" interview also gave Black Bart an excellent platform for continuing the story of his charade family. Protecting his own family of which he was proud and one of whom, E. A. Boles, Miller probably knew in his own first days in Yreka in 1854/55. But by 1888 his son E.A. was in El Dorado Co. CA and his brothers A.B. and J.W. were in Douglas Co. Nevada. And, no doubt at Alvy Boles expense, he brought his son Emery to California in 1853 at the age of 12 and later Emery was joined in Nevada by J. W. another son.

The 1840 census is the last census that had Alvy Boles living with his wife Dorcas. In 1850 census Alvy was then in California and professing to be a widower. It seems that they may have moved elsewhere near other relatives after Alvy's Mother's death. But then came news of the Gold Rush in California and Alvy arrived there in 1849 no doubt leaving behind an again pregnant wife. But Dorcas, who seems to have married a Gordon, also previously married, and they raised their previous progeny together except for one of Alvy's daughters, who seems to have been raised in another household. Eventually Dorcas Boles Gordon died. No doubt Alvy Boles had sent money to Dorcas all along and perhaps some Wells Fargo money shipments had gone awry.

Chapter 30

Douglas Co. Nevada

Joaquin Miller's "What Bart Says" edition sparked interest and memories elsewhere. For on Dec. 4, 1888 Carson City's *Nevada Tribune* published an article saying "There is no longer any doubt as to the notorious Black Bart being in this part of the state, as he was recognized in Reno by several persons, especially railroad detectives."

Naturally, or strangely, the *Nevada Tribune* wrote nothing about any connection between Black Bart and Alvy Boles whose son E. A. Boles had a blacksmith shop in Genoa, Nevada since around 1870. But also E.A. had property in Placerville, CA. where Alvy Boles had also originally mined. Perhaps like everyone else, the *Nevada Tribune* chose not to embarrass local citizens who had done no wrong or they honestly were ignorant of the connections.

We hear nothing more from Joaquin Miller or anyone else about Alvy Boles until Alvy Boles death notices began to appear. First his sons E.A. and J.W. gave notice of his death appearing in The *Reno Stockman and Gazetteer,* Reno, N V listing his death in Jan, 1890, in Placerville, Ca. Followed by other notices in The *Mountain Democrat* Placerville, CA and The *Yreka Journal*, Yreka, CA

For Miller, Alvy Boles's passing in January1890 must have been the beginning of another sad year of reflection as he was losing so many ties to his own past. How sad when he was last rooted on his own "Hights" above Oakland, California and he could see the whole Bay Area just as Frémont saw it when he had camped there, and as Miller first saw it when he visited there with other San Francisco journalists. But now Frémont, who wrote the report that Joaquin's father read to them before setting out for the West, was gone too

Did Miller first learn of Alvy Boles' death from Judge Rosborough who had been living in Oakland since long before Miller? Or was it from Edwin Markham whom you remember first met Alvy Boles when Markham was 16 or so and tending sheep over Mendocino way? Or maybe it wasn't until March 1890 that someone sent Miller a clipping from an Yreka newspaper wherein Robert Nixon Jr. told all too tersely in one paragraph of the passing of Alvy Boles in Placerville, CA on January 1890. And how he had sold potatoes at a fair price.

This was the same Robert Nixon Jr. who was in Yreka at the same time as young E. A. Boles, and who was listed as editor when it published the 1885 Yreka General Register. This register still listed Alvy Boles as a blacksmith in Yreka when he actually was in San Quentin as C.E. Boles.

The "What Bart Says" interview had given Black Bart the opportunity to carry on his charade narrative about his so-called family whose saga strangely mirrored that of his own real family. He wrote to many people from San Quentin and he answered many who wrote to him. But no record has been found of his visiting any of them after his release.

Chapter 31

Retrospection

By 1892 Joaquin Miller was enjoying the success of his past literary productions, but feeling more and more the loss of past companions, and enmeshed again in bad family publicity and he turned to eulogizing the past and trying to set history straight.

Every California school child was learning Miller's poem "Columbus," which he wrote for $50.00 for Mrs. Leslie for her promotion of the 1893 Columbian Exposition. Congress had declared a National holiday to celebrate the landing of Columbus on San Salvador Island thus beginning of our present Columbus Day. And Miller's poem "Columbus" was appearing everywhere: in "Christopher Columbus and His Monument Columbia 1892 Compiled by J.M. Dickey; in No. 36. Standard Recitations by Best Authors. Compiled by Frances P. Sullivan; America's Recitation Book. Compiled by Caroline B. Le Row.

But for Miller, again there was more bad family publicity. The *Sacramento Daily Union* (Jan. 8/82) rptd. from the San Francisco papers: "Harry Miller, son of Joaquin Miller, the 'Poet of the Sierras,' was sentenced to two years imprisonment today for holding up a stage in Mendocino County some weeks ago."

For a while Miller went to live near San Diego. And he mailed a letter to [William Hayes] Ward from Tijuana, Mexico, just across the border from San Diego Jan. 13/92.

Otherwise Miller's books were enjoying numerous reprints with only slight revisions and additions: Chicago's Morrill, Higgins and Company did *The Danites in the Sierras,* and *My Life Amongst the Modocs. My Life Amongst the Indians,* (The Midland Series) and *Songs of the Sierras and Sunlands* (Two Volumes in One . . .) and *Songs of Summer Lands.* 1892 *Mother, and Other Poems,* Boston and New York, 1892 [Cam. List].

Some of his poems were being sung with music; "Beyond Jordan" from Songs of the Sun-Lands as "He Blessed Them" a Song for Children's Sunday [School].

"How We Hung Red Shield." in Werner's Readings and Reflections No. 7. Compiled and arranged by Elsie M. Wilbor. New York: Edgar S. Werner & Co. 1892

Miller's 1892 *The Building of the City Beautiful.* Chicago: Stone & Kimball. [PMC only, gives 1892--see 1893.]

One personal bright spot of the year for Miller would have been another visit from Mrs. Frank Leslie. But it didn't happen. Mrs. Frank Leslie, who had married C.K.W. Wilde - brother of Miller's friend Oscar Wilde, and 100 journalists left N.Y. City by train for the first annual convention of the International Press Club in San Francisco. Everywhere she was interviewed along the way she recited Miller's poem "Columbus." She was eager to see Miller again in San Francisco but he was in San Diego when she was there in San Francisco.

1892 was also the year that, Adolphe de Castro, W.C. Morrow and Miller formed the Western Authors Publishing Company with the idea of issuing their own works. But Bierce's poetry book *Black Beetles in Amber* was the only thing they published. Note it included "Black Bart PO8" and "The Convicts Ball."

As for Miller, he had started doing a series of historical and reflective pieces on people he had known for the San Francisco *Morning Call.* Loring Pickering was still an owner and editor [newspapers in 1892 also give Charles Greene as an editor but he was still then editor of *Overland Monthly*] as David Spreckels and Charles Shortridge didn't become owners until 1896.

Miller's San Francisco *Morning Call* articles began in a sort of biographical way beginning April 24 with "Fighting Indians." "The Warfare of Early Days in Eastern Oregon." Followed in May by "A California Hero: Hugh Slicer and His Career in the Golden State" and "Mount Shasta on Fire." May 8, and "How we found I-DA-HO" May 22, and "Pony Express Riders." [Ike Mossman] May 29/92. "Across the Plains: Pioneers Who Made the Overland Journey" in the San Francisco *Morning Call* June 5 was followed by "Bret Harte defended by Joaquin Miller."

And lastly in his 1908 *Pacific Monthly* story, "Tales of Bad Men and Frontiersmen" Joaquin Miller's story of Black Bart was probably as he wanted us to remember Black Bart and he left it to historians and Black Bart's descendants to honor in memory the real frontiersman Alvy Boles. Miller wrote:

"But the most notable and famous stage-robber ever found in California never carried a gun; that is, never carried any ball or powder. That was Black Bart, the gentleman poet highwayman. For years he had things his own way, never shot at anyone, didn't want to hurt anybody, and so carried an old gun as guiltless of danger as an old walking stick. And he was never fired upon by the express guard but once. But, as always must and will happen, he was overthrown at last. This gentleman poet robber dropped his handkerchief one night, after a five-thousand-dollar haul. This had the laundryman's mark on it. This laundry was located in San Francisco and the gentleman poet robber was found in his elegant rooms, leading the life of a capitalist. As he had hidden away quite a sum of treasure, he was allowed to make terms with the company, being already an aged man, and was sent to the penitentiary for the short period of five years. It was his habit to leave some lines of verse in the treasure box after sacking it, and some of it was not at all bad. I recall only one verse. After some debate with himself about the situation as he lies in the chaparral waiting for the stage, he says:

> "But come what may I'll try it on,
> My fortunes can't be worse,
> And if there's money in that box
> It's money in my purse."

As this man had signed my name to some of his verses, and as I try to see all sorts of original characters, so that I may learn what I can as I go through life, I wrote and asked the warden of San Quentin for permission to spend a few days in the prison, so that I might see and study Black Bart. I was graciously asked to come on and had a hearty welcome. I found Black Bart in his shirt sleeves, smoking a good cigar and officiating as clerk of the drug store. He had nothing of the air or appearances of the convict about him and spoke cheerily about the kindness of his keepers and his hopes of soon returning to his home in New York.

"Don't want to go on the road any more?"

"Stage-robbing is the poorest trade in the United States, and I think I know the trade from Alpha to Omega. It is as poor pay as writing poetry.... Wasn't you ever a stage-robber? Then the newspapers have lied about you."

I told him that I was none too good to rob a few, but had never yet tackled one. He laughed and then said, seriously: `No man in his senses would ever try to be a robber. I had been sick for a long time, tried once to kill myself, then decided to hold up stage. It was as easy as slipping off a log. But you see where it must end, does always end. No, I don't know as I am particularly sorry. I never hurt nobody and the express is only a robber, a very rich robber, that is all. I am only telling you it don't pay; nothing in it; capture only a matter of time.'

I have always entertained the idea that any man in this free land of great opportunities, who embarks on a career of crime, must be a bit unsound. And this man, as he says, was not in health, and of course his sense of all things was more or less warped. But I was disappointed to find him not at all penitent. He laughed about his poetry, but was glad to have me praise one or two points in it, and said he was writing something much better. When I left the prison he gave me several small poems which I have mislaid somewhere in these last twenty years, and he promised to accept my invitation to make my cabin his home for a while after his release; but he never came. Maybe he forgot his promise. Anyhow, I am quite certain he was a little off his balance, to say the least." (Miller: "Tales of Bad Men and Frontiersmen" *Pacific Monthly* 19.1, Jan.1908).

Alvy Boles lived from 1811 to 1890 and Joaquin Miller lived from 1839 to 1913. Both were part of the Gold Rush and westernization of the United States of America. Boles became a Celebrity by becoming Black Bart and Joaquin Miller became a Celebrity by being socially and politically incorrect at nearly every turn and only now, nearly a century after Miller's death, is he becoming understood as an historian of his times.

Miller went to the gold fields as a boy of fifteen, lived on and off with the *Wintu* Indians for four or more years, wounded a constable, stole a horse, escaped jail, studied law, became a pony express rider, bought an interest in a newspaper only to have it closed by the govt. because of his seditious editorials, wrote poetry, practiced law, fought and killed Indians, was accused of adultery and obtained a divorce because of his wife's adultery, associated with judges and criminals alike, questioned the positions of icons of his day, wrote on both sides of the Chinese question, and opened up subjects such as racism and race extermination.

Men and women of all walks of life honored Alvy Boles by never disclosing his other identity as the Real Black Bart.

Joaquin Miller honored himself and all people by composing one simple stanza using the code by which he lived and, as usual, borrowing from an article he had written earlier-"Old Baboon." Remember?

> "In Men whom men condemn as ill
> I find so much of goodness still,
> In men whom men pronounce divine
> I find so much of sin and blot,
> I hesitate to draw a line
> Between the two where God has not.

****

Epilogue

Today's 2016 Wikipedia highlights Black Bart as C.E. Boles from stories written by people who didn't know or read Joaquin Miller nor Ambrose Bierce.

Bill O'Reilly's Lies and Legends used a plethora of books embellishing misconceptions built on earlier fabrications from misconstructions of Joaquin Millers work by jealous journalists who hadn't been there.

Stage coach robberies literally became newspaper front page news as soon as stage coaches started running. Black Bart was perhaps California's most notorious stage coach robber. He robbed 29 times from Wells Fargo boxes on the coaches from 1875 until 1883. Two in Southern Oregon the rest in Northern California.

This story takes you back to 1888 where Joaquin Miller wrote after Barts release "What Bart Says" December 2, 1888, the San Fransisco Examiner. On that date Joaquin Miller, chose to use the name Bolton for Black Bart, one of the names under which Bart had been arrested, as Miller was still covering for Alvy Boles and where Alvy was.

Collins and Levene 1992 *Black Bart* (contents pp 14-17) listing of the robberies and their maps showed that the robberies were all in areas where Alvy Boles had originally lived, operated mule pack train, and would often visit friends he had known in earlier days.

Numerous books have been written about Black Bart. Many

of which include the canard that Black Bart was afraid of horses. Which is ridiculous when we find out that Black Bart had been a blacksmith most of his life.

Roy Morris, Jr in his 1995 *Ambrose Bierce Alone in Bad Company (p. 137)* continued literary academia's misconceptions about Joaquin Miller when he wrote:

> Even Joaquin Miller, the self-styled "poet on the Sierras," whom everyone in San Francisco considered something of a joke, had taken his one-man Wild West show to England and been received with great applause, if only in the nature of children tossing peanuts to a monkey on a stick. As a literary gold mine, San Francisco was pretty much played out; London was a never ending vein of ore.

But the miners who went to California after the discovery of gold there in "49" read Joaquin Miller well as they settled into their new lives in the Far West.

The real story was, many like Alva Bowles [Alvy Boles] and Justin Hinckley Sisson (1826 1893) were led by fellow Indian miners further north to the Mt. Shasta area gold fields. Alva Bowles [Alvy Boles] was first mining in Major Reading's land grant in todays Shasta County in 1850. There he was accused, tried, and acquitted of killing another miner as it was proven that one of Ben Wright's Oregon Indians had done the murder.

Boles and his fellow miners were led further north by their Indian friends on what is now known as Old Stage Road past todays Mt. Shasta Sisson Museum and on north along this ancient Indian trail crossing today's Boles Creek in Weed, continuing north through today's Edgewood and on eventually to the Klamath River in Oregon.

I last visited that museum in October 2013 where I delivered a speech on the subject of *Joaquin Miller and the Real Black Bart*. My first visit had been with my grandmother Florence May Sisson-Guilford when the museum building had been a fish hatchery, where we went to see the large sturgeons swimming in the outdoor pools.

My Civil War veteran grandfather, Andrew Johnson Guilford (1838-1915) could have known any Boles that mined in Idaho, while trying his hand at mining after the Civil War.

Many of these 49ers became part of the development of California and avid readers of the local newspapers as they knew the people and places written about. Thus they could all read between Miller and Bierce's lines.

The publisher, George Hearst, who had early mining interest and a summer home on the McCloud River, knew both well Joaquin Miller and Alvy Boles. Joaquin miller, like everyone else, recognized the 1883 picture of the captured Black Bart not as C.E. Boles, the confessed Black Bart, but as the Alvy Boles he had known since the 1850's.

When Alvy Boles died in 1890, word reached Joaquin Miller and Ambrose Bierce. They both reminisced about their visit to Alvy Boles when he was in San Quentin and their relationship with him during Boles's Siskiyou years. And so Miller wrote in *The Wasp*, where Ambrose Bierce usually published his own work, a poem which was probably Millers first eulogy to Boles in December 13, 1890, entitled;

Is it Worth While?

Is it worth while that we jostle a brother
    In bearing his load on the rough road of life?
  Is it worth while that we jest at each other

In blackness of heart- that we war to the knife?
God pity us all in our pitiful strife.
God pity us all as we jostle each other;
God pardon us all for the triumphs we feel
When a fellow goes down 'neath his load on the heather
Pierced to the heart. Words are keener than steel,
And mightier far for woe than for weal.
Were it not well, in this brief little journey,
On over the Isthmus, down into the tide,
We give him a fish instead of a serpent,
Ere folding his hands to be and abide
Forever and aye in [the] dust at his side?
Look at the roses saluting each other;
Look at the herd all at peace on the plain;
Man and man only, makes war on his brother
And laughs in his heart at his peril and pain,
Shamed by the beasts that go down on the plain.
Is it worth while that we battle to humble
Some poor fellow down into dust?
God pity us all! Time too soon will humble
All of us together, like leaves in a gust
Humbled, indeed, down into dust.

Later in July of 1892, Joaquin Miller wrote in the *San Francisco Morning Call* **How We Struck It** ... "Names were rare luxuries in those days, especially long ones like this, and many a good old man may be found in those mountains to this day with name and date and nationality all worn away and gone as from an old quarter. But the true silver, trust God, is still there." Was this Miller's second tribute to the recently departed Alvy Boles, whom the detectives, and history have recorded as C.E. Boles? Hearst would have known that Alvy Boles was the one who had really given Joaquin Miller his first "pointer" in looking for gold near Boles Mine and Horse Creek.

Since, Joaquin Miller's relative John F. Miller was California's first Senator and George Hearst would become its second Senator, arranging for Hearst's two well-known S.F. journalists, Miller and Bierce, to overnight at San Quentin and interview the confessed Black Bart was no problem.

As Collins and Bruce Levene so well chronicled in their "Spurious" (fictional) section of their *Black Bart.* Reprints from the daily *Examiner* show titillating correspondence between Hearst and Miller giving their readers tid-bits regarding a possible interview with recently released Black Bart.

Miller's interview signed as "Martin" (the same alias as used by Black Bart while he was at the Reader Ranch) could have been written from anywhere as it was over trails and with people well known to both Miller and Black Bart.

I too have traveled those trails and talked with Indian descendants of those ranchers as we ate at our table overlooking the McCloud River.

Alvy Boles (Black Bart) died in 1890 and he was buried in Placerville, CA. His well-known sons put a one line notice, signed with just their initials, in the Nevada papers. Then the Yreka, CA paper's editors, who had known Boles for nearly all their California lives, also eulogized Alvy Boles only as "the man who had sold potatoes to the miners at fair prices during the starving times."

Joaquin Miller died in 1913 and Ambrose Bierce disappeared in Mexico in 1914. No one seems to have written about the many times both men had visited George Hearst's vast Mexican ranch.

It wasn't until 1916, three years after Miller died, that George Wharton James in his "Exposition Memories San Diego 1916", & "The Radiant Life Press, 1917" That Markham disclosed to him that his *Mendocino Memory* was written about the area in which he had meet Black Bart with his mule pack train on the trail in Mendocino County.

Remember Edwin Markham, Ambrose Bierce, Frank Norris, Fremont Older, and Ina Coolbrith were frequent visitors to Joaquin Miller's "Hights". So they had to have known about Alvy Boles and Black Bart.

It is perhaps a memorial to the civility of the basic culture of those early days that the Indians always lost Black Bart's tracks, and none of his contemporaries ever wrote or spoke Bart's real name, Alvy Boles, when they were writing or speaking of the real Black Bart. Because they knew him and his family and they were protecting them. He had served his time.

Only today Bill O'Reilly has admitted Black Bart was a real unknown, namely because O'Reilly never had all this research presented to him.

Even when Harr Wagner wrote one of the first biography on Miller in 1929, he recorded the fact that Alva Boles gave Miller his first mining tip in the winter months of 53-54. Which verifies Millers reference to Black Bart as an early mining acquaintance.

Originally I thought possibly the article was by Harr L Wagner, but it was Harry L Wells who rode back to Shasta Valley in 1883 to see Edward Allison, who told him it was Alva Boles who had given Joaquin Miller his first mining tip.

The Kentuckian was Edward Allison, born in Madison County, Kentucky in 1809. He was at Deer Creek Nevada City, Nevada County, California at the same time as Alva Boles. This is the Kentuckian referred to by Harry L Wells writing in the newspaper (Signed HLW) after Bart's capture and photograph in 1883. Edward Allison is Great grandfather of Eric Vollmers who is now collaborating with me on an Indian Trails book.

Future historians would do well to chase Joaquin Miller's excellent newspaper articles signed with the pseudonyms like "Esmerelda" one in the Boise paper which led to the photo exposé of the real Black Bart.

I thank God for having put all of these "Clewes" in my path and for granting me these extra years so that I can finish this manuscript.

Appendix I

The Lost Cabin

One of the Legends of Northern California.
The Gold Mine That Was Guarded by a
Grizzly-How It Was Found and How It
Was Lost Thirty Years Ago.
[Written for the Sunday *Call*.]

The "Lost Cabin" is a legend of Northern California and Southern Oregon, as elusive as an *ignis fatuus* and unsubstantial as a dream; the first thing to salute the ear of a stranger and the last about which he can gather any satisfactory information; something of which more is said and less known than any other of the many interesting topics of pioneer days, over which the "old timers" nightly dispute as they sit around the pine log fire in the hotel bar room, or gather in select groups in the back rooms of some old comrade's store. It is a legend in which vivid imagination and an absence of that strict regard for verifiable facts which should mark the chronicler, have builded upon a slender foundation of facts a tale as varied and different as the relators. These stories are legion, and in trying to reconcile them or at least trace them back to a common ancestry, the writer has spent many a patient hour, with no result save to gather into his storehouse of undigested notes a miscellaneous assortment of "lost cabin" stories covering the country from the Sacramento to the Umpqua like a plaster, so numerous that were they realities, the difficulty would be to avoid these decaying shanties rather than to find their whereabouts. But one of the many narrators has laid claim to positive personal information and his version of the story has been accepted as the original and only "lost cabin" story, and all others are hereby declared to be frauds and delusions.

It was early in his researches that the writer was advised to interview old Alvy Boles. Upon inquiring who that individual might be and where he was to be found, he learned that he was an itinerant blacksmith and generally made his headquarters at a certain ranch in Shasta Valley. Procuring a light buggy the scribe drove from Yreka to the valley and found the object of his search, a tall, rawboned Kentuckian, apparently about seventy years of age.

Old Boles's Story

Relieved of the numerous interrogatories necessary to draw it out, and stripped of the vehement invective and tedious repetitions, the "lost cabin" story as then related by Mr. Boles is substantially as follows:

In the good old days of 1850, before California had yet become a state and while the excitement over the Trinity mines was raging furiously, there stood on the trail from Shasta to Weaverville a large canvas structure kept as a public house and known far and wide as the "Blue Tent." Here, for the moderate sum of one dollar, the weary traveler could procure a meal of bacon, beans, and coffee, and allay his thirst with villainous whiskey at two bits a drink. Another dollar secured for him the privilege of spreading his blankets upon the ground floor and sleeping until it was time to squander a third dollar for breakfast, consisting chiefly of what was left over from supper, and attractively spread upon slabs beneath the stalwart pines. The Blue Tent had its counterpart in every new mining camp, and it was no better nor worse than its fellows. It was a favorite rendezvous for miners, who nightly gathered there to participate in its revelries, try their luck at the gaming-tables, and swap lies with any who might have that commodity to barter.

Late In the Summer

There crossed the mountains a company from Indiana, having waved a tearful adieu to the land of hoop-poles and pumpkins and came to seek their fortune on the golden slope of the Sierra. Their long journey across the plains being over, and the necessity for union, which its perils and privations demanded, no longer existing, the company broke up into small bands and scattered in all directions. Among them were three warm friends whose homes were by the muddy current of the Wabash, and now that they were strangers in a distant land they resolved to unite their fortunes and court the smiles of the fickle goddess together.

Two of these, named Cox and Benedict, were men who had long since passed the golden age of youth, while the other, a son of Senator Compton, was still in the vigor of a young and hopeful manhood. Having decided to stick together, the next question that presented itself was one of a definite plan of operations. Should they go into the mines with pick, shovel, pan, and rocker, or should they embark in some business scheme where the profits were more sure, leaving to others the wet drudgery of the mines with its great possibilities and uncertainties. Like the great majority, they decided upon the former course and started for the Trinity mines, whose fame was then drawing thousands of new emigrants as well as experienced miners from the older diggings. At that time an "experienced miner" was one who had worked a few weeks and learned the rudiments of placer mining, for more than the rudiments were known by few in those restless, exciting, experimental days.

In furtherance of this decision they reached the Blue Tent on their way to Weaverville. Here they learned that the diggings on Trinity were overrun with men unable to find a paying claim, and that gold had been discovered on Klamath, Salmon, and other streams to the north, whither many were going notwithstanding the hostile spirit displayed by the savages of that region. This intelligence worked a change in their plans and led them to determine upon a general prospecting trip to the north, passing into a region about which little was known save that THE NATIVES WERE WARLIKE AND AGGRESSIVE. Paying but little heed to the mournful predictions that they would find but little gold and that their scalps would soon assist in the interior decorations of some brave Indian's wigwam, they laid in a liberal stock of provisions, and with their blankets strapped upon their shoulders and the supplies and utensils up-on the back of a diminutive and long-suffering mule, they turned their faces northward and resolutely plunged into the unknown wilderness beyond.

Notwithstanding the hardships incipient to a journey into a

strange country, over high mountains and through deep canons, during which they lost their mule by a stampede and sustained a compound fracture of the cradle that was to have rocked them into a competency, they finally reached in their wandering the headwaters of the north fork of Trinity River. In their numerous prospects many times "color" had been found, but nothing that gave promise of yielding the wealth they had set their minds upon, and so they still journeyed on in search of "pound diggings."

An Exploring Tour

One evening camp was pitched on the side of a small mountain, where a cold spring bubbled up between the spreading roots of a giant pine. It happened to be Compton's turn to attend to the camp duties and prepare the meals; and while the young man was engaged in gathering firewood and making preparations for the evening repast, his two elder companions started out upon a short tour of exploration.

Left alone to his work the cook collected a pile of faggots, made a pot of hot coffee, some water biscuits, and fried a skillet of bacon whose savory smell made him long for the speedy return of his associates. At last hunger overcame his sense of etiquette and he sat down alone to the tempting repast, hoping the others would soon join him. In this he was disappointed, for the supper became cold and darkness settled down upon the mountain without any sign of their presence being given.

Compton became uneasy. He began to fear that something unusual had happened. They might have perished at the hands of Indians without any warning of a struggle reaching him, for an arrow is a noiseless missile, and even the repeat of a rifle could be kept from his ears by the intervening hills and the dense forest. On the side of the mountain, some distance above the camp and where the hill was comparatively barren, was an immense ledge of rocks, and the idea of building upon this a beacon fire to guide his friends homeward in case they had lost their way, suggested itself to his mind and was quickly acted upon. It also occurred to him that in case hostile savages were about, the camp fire was calculated to make him altogether too conspicuous.

He decided to leave it, and after building his beacon light, to retire some distance into the shadow and see whether it attracted friends and foes. It was but the work of a few minutes to pile upon the ledge an immense heap of dry brush; but just as he was about to ignite it he heard the voices of his friends calling to him from the camp below, whither they had just returned and were surprised to find it deserted. Leaving the useless beacon unlit, which stands to-day as a landmark to assure him who is so fortunate as to find it that the "lost cabin" is close by. Compton hastened down the hill, eager to learn why his companions had so long delayed their return. It was a most wonderful story they poured into his astonished ears.

The Grizzly and the Gold

In their ramble they wandered some distance from camp, careful, however, to keep their bearings so that they could return without difficulty, and finally came upon a beaten trail, apparently made by animals, along which they travelled leisurely for some distance. Suddenly, just as they rounded a point of rocks, a huge grizzly bear rose up from the bushes immediately in front of them. His shaggy form looked massive and terrible, while the ferocious growl plainly showed that something had occurred to sour his temper. They had never seen a grizzly before, but had heard many stories of his great size, strength and ferocity, and knew at once that the animal that now disputed their passage was the great monarch of the mountains himself, and that to run was useless. Without stopping to speak or even to see what the other was going to do, each whipped out his revolver and poured shot after shot into the shaggy breast and open mouth of the brute, and by one or two lucky shots succeeded in dispatching the monster before he had time to realize that these strange animals that walked on their hind legs and spit fire, really intended to fight him.

When he fell to the ground they turned and congratulated each other upon their lucky escape, and then cautiously approached their fallen adversary to see what a dead grizzly really looked like. They found him lying in a hole several feet in diameter and partially filled with lava rock. Having satisfied themselves that their late antagonist was dead, they leaped into the hole intent upon securing some bear meat for breakfast; and while carving for their anticipated meal, one of them noticed a peculiar object in the hole and stooped to pick it up. It proved to be a little lump of gold.

Bear steaks were forgotten, while the two victorious hunters began pitching out the lava rock with feverish haste. A small space was soon cleared and the loose dirt at the bottom was found to be literally studded with lumps of gold of various sizes, enough to make them rich and ensure their comfort for the remainder of their days. Gathering darkness warned them to return to camp while yet there was light to guide them, and carefully marking the spot so that it could again be found, they hastened back to their companion, bearing sample nuggets to verify their wonderful tale.

Building the Cabin

They sat late over the flickering camp-fire, laying plans for the future, wondering how much of the precious metal that astonishing hole contained, and seeking in vain for some plausible theory to account for its presence there at all. At last, completely tired out, they fell asleep while visions of Sinbad's wonderful valley of diamonds and the marvelous riches produced by the genius of Aladdin's lamp, floated before their slumber-wrapped eyes. Camp was moved in the morning to the vicinity of the wonderful hole where the grizzly had been slain, and they made deliberate preparations to reap their golden harvest. Six hundred paces east of where the bear lay they constructed two small cabins, one for themselves and one for their possessions.

They worked a short time and then decided to build a larger and more comfortable house in which to spend the winter months and began cutting the logs for that purpose; but as winter approached with its unknown dangers of Indians, scarcity of food and possible burial by snow they concluded to abandon their discovery and go out of the mountains. Their mining tools and camping outfit were carefully stowed away in one of the cabins, where they still remain to testify to the truth of this story.

They blazed their way on the trees as they went along, and in due time arrived at the Blue Tent, where they convinced the croakers that their scalps still perched upon their craniums and that there was an abundance of gold to be found in the unknown regions of the north. They made no secret of their success, freely exhibiting their dust and nuggets, and telling everyone how they had been secured.

From the Blue Tent they proceeded to San Francisco, whence Cox and Benedict sailed for their home on the banks of the Wabash, satisfied with their moderate fortune, while young Compton remained to seek again in the spring the abandoned treasure. During the winter he was stricken with the cholera morbus, and though cared for tenderly by a fellow Mason named Maxwell, died in a few days. Before his death the young man gave explicit directions to his fraternal friend how to reach the auriferous hole in the far mountains of the Trinity.

The Cabin Lost

Early in the spring, party after party started out in search of the deserted cabins, some of them having directions given Maxwell, but most of them "going it blind." Knowing simply, in an indefinite kind of a way, that somewhere to the northward there were wonderful diggings, near which would be found an empty cabin. In vain hundreds of men searched through the mountains, the cabins could not be found and they have remained completely lost to the present day.

For a number of years a few hopeful ones made periodical excursions in search of the elusive cabins, but gradually the tale of the wonderful pit of gold, guarded by its huge dragon, the grizzly, was relegated to the catalogue of marvelous legends in which the early history of California is so rich; yet even now can occasionally be found a credulous man who is inclined to believe there is "something in it," and old Alvy Boles, the only true and faithful devotee, annually studies his faded memorandum, and then visits the headquarters of the Trinity, to search for the grizzly's grave with as much zeal as did good Sir Lancelot for the Holy Grail. H.L.W. (*The San Francisco Morning Call* Sunday, December 16, 1883. Vol. LV (16):1:3, 4.)

Bibliography of Margaret Guilford-Kardell's Research

Asbill, Frank and Shawley, Argle, *The Last of the True West*, A Hearthstone Book. Carlton Press, Inc., New York, N.Y.1975.

Asbill, Frank. Frank Asbill's Map, courtesy of Jill Kane, Great, great granddaughter of Pierce Asbill.

Atherton, Gertrude, *My San Francisco*......1940

Carranco, Lynwood and Beard Estle, *Genocide and Vendetta: The Round Valley Wars of Northern California* .University of Oklahoma Press, Norman, OK

Collins, William and Levene, Bruce, *Black Bart: The True Story of The West's Most Famous Stagecoach Robber*. Pacific Transcriptions, Mendocino, California, 1992. pp. 272. Pacific Transcriptions, P.O. Box 526 Mendocino, CA 95460.

Cummins, Sarah J., *Autobiography and Reminiscences,* La Grande, Oregon (1914?) Chap. VIII).

Cuthill, Mrs. Lucie, "Historic Jenner School District." *Sonoma Historical Society, 1963 Journal,* Vol. 1 No. 2, March.   P.2.   Santa Rosa, CA.

Cutler, Phoebe, "Joaquin Miller and the Social Circle at the Hights." C*alifornia* History (*The Journal of the California Historical Society*, Vol. 90, No 1, November 2012, p57.)

Didion, Joan, *Where I Was From.* Alfred A. Knoff, New York, 2003 p. 83-84.

Frank, B.F., and Chappell H.W. *History and Business Directory of Shasta County 1881*, Redding, Ca. Redding Independent Book and Job Printing

Guilford-Kardell, Margaret and Dotta, James, *Occasional Papers No.1* Redding 1980

Guilford-Kardell, Margaret, "Joaquin Miller and Black Bart: Two Famous Shasta County Gold Miners." Address given at the Mar. 13, 1998 meeting of the Shasta Historical Society, Redding, CA.

Guilford-Kardell, Margaret and McKeown, Scott, *Margaret Guilford-Kardell's Bibliography on the Life, Times, and Exploits of Cincinnatus Hiner Miller*: http://www.joaquinmiller.com).

Hoeper, George, *Black Bart: Boulevardier Bandit.* Word Dancer Press 1995,950 N. Van Ness P.O. Box 4638, Fresno CA 93744-4638, p. 16, 18, 27, 29, 30,31,71,89,120, 157-160.

James, George Wharton, *Exposition Memories San Diego 1916*. The Radiant Life Press 1917, p. 62

Keter, Thomas S. "Early Trails of Southwestern Trinity County" May 1998. (Submitted to *Trinity County Historical Society*) (Reedited and published on solararch.org. February 2009).

Lewis, H. *A History of Northern California: A Memorial and a Biographical History*. 1891Chicago, H. Lewis Doubleday Publishing Co., 1891, p.243

Markham,

Miller, Cincinnatus Hiner, Joaquin and a collection of various other pseudonym: See

Parrish, Rev. E. E. Parrish, *Diary of Rev. Edward Evans Parrish: Crossing the Plains in 1844.* Ye Galleon Press, Fairfield, Washington 1988, p. 6.

Penfield, Thomas *Directory of Buried or Sunken Treasure and Lost Mines of the United States.* 1971 True Treasures Publications, Inc., P.O. Drawer L. Conroe, Texas 77301

Rosenus, Alan

("Excerpts from the Siskiyou County Comprehensive Land & Resource Management Plan February 1996" Klamath Bucket Brigade??). Siskiyou Co.

Slocum, Bowen & Co. Publishers *History of Napa and Lake Counties 1881*, Slocum,

Smith, Dottie, "Dottie Smith's Blog." Redding Record Searchlight Nov. 31, 2012

Southern, Mae Hazel [Elsewhere May], Typed Unpublished Manuscripts on file at the Redding, California Library 1948.

U. S. Census data 1850 -1930.

Wagner, Harr

Wendt, Ingrid & Primus, St. John. "Elizabeth Markham." *From Here We Speak: An Anthology of Oregon Poetry.* (Oregon Literature Series: v.4, Poetry, Gen. ed. George Venn, Managing ed. Ulrich H. Hardt) Corvallis Oregon: Oregon State U. Press, 1993p. 36

Wells, Harry L. *History of Siskiyou County, California 1881*, D. J. Stewart & Co. Oakland, CA pp. 240.

*****

Also see Bruce Levene's bibliography of his research for his 1992 book Black Bart.

Personal Communications:

David Boles, Great, great grandson of Alvy Boles.

Jill Kane, Great, Great granddaughter of Pierce Asbill

Linda Markham Curry Great Great grandniece of Edw. Markham

Ed Clouet

Jimmy Simas, Great grandson of Jeremiah Davidson

Index

A

Ah-Di-Na 33
Albro, George 44, 61, 118
Allison, Edward 171
Alturas 15, 17, 18, 19, 24, 95
American Ranch 32
Anderson 32, 101
Annibal xiv, 15, 18, 19, 24
Applegates 5
Arbuckle 111
Arcata 92
Asbill
    Elizabeth 27, 186
    Pierce 24, 25, 26, 27, 60, 62, 64, 97, 183, 186
Aull 108, 150, 152

B

Bablaine, Peter (Old Baboon) 7, 165
Backbone Ridge 43, 95
Baid xiii, xiv
Baker Brothers 65
Bancroft, Hubert Howe 129
Bannock City 20
Bass Hill 43, 94, 101, 103, 107, 119
B.B. (Blacksmith Bard) 44
Beachy, Hill 81
Berry Creek 92
Bierce, Ambrose i, 6, 13, 14, 39, 82, 122, 127, 132, 133, 166, 167, 168, 170, 171
Big Bend 47, 71
Big River 24, 25
Big Valley 90
Black Bart i, viii, ix, x, xi, xii, xiii, xiv, 1, 2, 4, 5, 7, 23, 26, 27, 29, 30, 31, 42, 44, 45, 53, 56, 57, 59, 60, 61, 62, 63, 64, 67, 71, 72, 73, 74, 75, 80, 85, 92, 93, 94, 96, 97, 98, 101, 102, 103, 107, 108, 109, 110, 111, 112, 113, 114, 115, 116, 117, 118, 119, 121, 122, 123, 127, 128, 129, 132, 133, 135, 137, 138, 139, 141, 142, 146, 147, 148, 152, 153, 154, 156, 157, 158, 159, 161, 162, 163, 164, 165, 166, 167, 168, 170, 171, 172, 183, 184, 186
Black Nicaraguan (speaking Spanish) 9
Bledsoe 13, 14
Bodega 26, 90, 91, 111, 123
Bogus 86, 87, 126
Boles
    Carrie (Caroline) 112
    C.E. viii, 60, 114, 116, 123, 132, 133, 147, 153, 159, 166, 168, 169
    Charles Everett 67
    David Lee xii, 67
    E.A. (Emery Allison) 38, 66, 71, 72, 101, 117, 123, 157, 158
    Harry or Henry Elsworth 90
    J.W. 72, 157, 158
    Leland Woodrow 67
Boles Creek 11, 38, 48, 167
Bolton, C.E., Carlos E., Charles 60, 61, 63, 67, 72, 96, 111, 114, 115, 116, 117, 121
Bonneville 83
Bowen, Jack 108
Bowles 30, 38, 42, 100, 167
Brewster 102, 103
Bridgeport 88, 106
Brock Creek 14, 43, 48, 82, 95, 139
Brock, James (Jim) x, xi, 4, 23, 37, 43, 44, 50, 70, 89, 95, 138, 139
Buckeye 94
Bullskin Ridge 15
Burgette 70, 100
Burgettville 100
Burney 102

Butler
    J.T. 14, 64
    T.S. 14
Butte 11, 21, 40, 81, 94
Butteville 11, 21, 38, 41, 48, 94, 119
Buzzard's Roost 102, 103

C

Cable, George Washington 124
Cahto 92
Calistoga 108
Callahan 109
Campbell
    Frank 41
    J.B. (Jeremiah) 139
Camptonville 106
Canyon City 6, 24, 125
Carson City 86, 158
Cassidy, Julie xi
Cedar Creek 14
Centerville 92, 93
Charleston 124
Chaucer, Geoffrey vi
Chenewas 47
Churntown 15, 35, 36
Clark, Frank 108
Clear Creek 30, 35, 42, 95
Clear Lake 27, 106
Clemens, Samuel (AKA Mark Twain) 102, 124, 136
Clouet, Ed xii, 186
Cloverdale 92, 106, 108, 110, 111
Cogswell, Lischen 22
Collins, William ix, 183
Colusa 65, 90, 93
Comptche 25
Coolbrith, Ina 68, 171
Copco Dam 86
Copper City 94, 95, 102
Copperopolis 80, 152
Cortez 54
Cottonwood 86, 90, 98
Cottonwood Creek 98
Covelo 25, 60, 62
Cow Creek 47, 48, 82
Crabtree, Lotta 6, 124
Crater Lake 11
Crescent City 5
Cuffey's Cove 24, 25
Cummins 22, 23, 37, 184

Curry, Linda Markham xii, 58, 186
Curtis, James 59
Cutler, Phoebe 68, 127, 184

D

Dairy Creek 11, 12
Davidson xiii, 4, 6, 19, 22, 23, 24, 37, 38, 61, 66, 98, 100, 186
De Blondey, Joe 31, 48
De Castro, Adolphe 161
Deer Creek 5, 171
Dickey, J.M. 160
Dobbins 105
Dog Creek 12, 32, 37, 38
Dog Town 32
Douglas County 72
Douglas, Frederick 136
Downieville 105
Dry Creek 123
Dunsmuir 32, 33, 138

E

Eagle Creek 98
Eaton 39
Eddings, Nort 99
Edgewood 11, 21, 38, 41, 48, 88, 94, 119, 167
Eilers
    D. 104
    Liepe 103
    Lu 103, 104
Elk 25
Emery, J.S. 69, 70
English 9, 24, 83, 108, 109, 123
Etna 98
Eugene 10, 20, 35
Evans x, 27, 115, 135, 185

F

Fall River 11, 23, 33, 37, 38, 43, 48, 49, 50, 51, 65, 70, 71, 86, 87, 88, 95, 96, 102, 103, 104, 119
Fall River Mills 11, 23, 65, 87, 88, 96, 102, 103, 104
Fall River Valley 38, 50, 51, 65, 71, 86, 95
Farnier, Frank (AKA Portuguese Frank) 13, 15, 16, 17, 18, 19, 20, 24, 25, 26, 27, 58, 60, 98
Fleming 115
Fletcher 25
Florence 22, 168
Forbestown 94

Forse, Henry 106
Fort Bragg, Cook, Jones, Ross xi, 27, 58, 90, 91, 98
Fox, Frank 95
Frank x, xii, 12, 13, 14, 15, 16, 17, 18, 19, 20, 24, 25, 26, 27, 28, 29, 30, 33, 37, 41, 44, 45, 58, 60, 61, 62, 63, 64, 73, 88, 95, 98, 100, 103, 104, 108, 109, 111, 124, 137, 161, 171, 183, 184
Freaner, James L. (Col.) 15, 40, 49, 82
Fruitvale 70
Funk Hill 76, 80

G

Genoa 66, 67, 71, 72, 76, 90, 101, 105, 117, 123, 158
Gertrude 118, 183
Geysers 108, 110
Gilliam, Martin 27
Girard Ridge 33
Glenburn 71, 96
Glendening 83
Golden Chariot Mine 81
Gonsalves, Louis 25
Gordon, Dorcas Boles xii, 70, 85, 157
Gray, John S. 128
Grayson, George 81
Gripenberg, Alexandra 136

H

Hackett, George 154
Harrington 43
Harrison Gulch 110
Harrison, W.R. 42, 110
Harte, Bret 162
Hastings 31
Hawes Ranch (Fort Ranch) 44
Hawkinsville 101
Hayfork 61
Hazel Creek 32
Hearst
    William Randolph 132, 137
Heenan, John 7
Helm, Dave (Old Tex) 12
Hibbs, Johnny 11
Higgins, Alex E. 32
Higginson, Thomas Wentworth 136
Hights 4, 68, 70, 125, 127, 136, 156, 159, 171, 184
Himes, William 71, 96
Hoeper, George 60, 135, 184

Hopland 106
Hornbrook 86, 99, 100
Horse Creek 28, 29, 87, 99, 170
Horsetown 30, 32, 90
Hostettler, J.H. 125
Huckleberry Creek 138
Humboldt xii, 26, 27, 90
Humbug xiii, 28, 29, 41, 49, 61, 84, 87, 99, 109, 139
Hume 92, 93, 108, 114, 115, 116, 136, 137, 140, 146, 147, 148, 149, 150, 151, 152, 156, 157
Hutton Creek 87

I

Ida Elmore Mine 81, 82
Indian Nancy 11

J

Jackass Flats 32
Jackson 49, 76, 99, 112
Jacksonville 5, 100, 101
James, George Wharton 57, 170, 185
Jenner, Gail viii, 114
Jernigan, Bob 115
Johnson, Rufus 38, 53, 59

K

Kane, Jill xii, 183, 186
Karuk Indians 70
Kelseyville 106
Kenyon, Frank 14
Keter, Thomas S. 185
Kingsley's Trading Post, Red Bluff 29
Klamath Bucket Brigade 33, 185
Klamath River 29, 70, 86, 87, 101, 167

L

Lake County 65, 92, 185
Lakeport 108, 110, 111, 154
Lamoine 12
Landrum, Joel T. 51
Lane, Joe 22, 40, 48
La Porte 92, 94, 107
Laytonville 90, 92
Legerton, Lou viii, 72, 114
Leslie, Frank 124, 161
Levene, Bruce ix, xi, xii, 100, 102, 105, 114, 170, 183, 186
Lewis, H. 185

Lewiston 14, 109
Little Lake 106
Lockhart
    Harry 37, 49, 109
    Sam 32, 37, 38, 48, 49, 50, 51, 81
Louisville 28, 65
Lovelock 28
Lower Lake 64, 107, 108
Lytle Flat 38

M

Magruder 81
Major Reading 14, 30, 32, 35, 37, 42, 167
Markham xii, xiv, 1, 20, 21, 23, 24, 28, 57, 58, 59,
        60, 61, 62, 67, 68, 74, 85, 109, 110, 117, 136,
        159, 170, 171, 185, 186
Marshall, Jack 109
Martin 27, 43, 44, 45, 88, 89, 118, 137, 138, 139,
        140, 157, 170
Marysville 80, 81, 85, 105
Mason xiii, 23, 68, 75, 111, 114, 117, 181
Matquaw Flats 35, 43
Mazzini, Joe xi, 103
McClintock, William King 126
McCloud River xi, 32, 33, 35, 42, 43, 49, 66, 115,
        124, 138, 139, 168, 170, 193
McCloud, Ross 33, 48
McComb 130
McConnell 152
McCreary 60
McDermitt 21, 22, 23, 40
McDougal 10
McElroy 50
McKay
    Donald 83
    Tom 83
Meek 83
Mendocino County xi, 26, 57, 64, 106, 160, 171
Mendocino Memory 57, 109, 171
Menken, Adah Isaacs 7
Middletown 32, 90, 108, 109
Miller
    C.H. (Cincinnatus Hiner) AKA Joaquin
            (Pseudonyms Esmeralda, Skurb, Etc)
            24, 49, 84
    George 22, 83
    Hulings 6, 22, 23, 70, 83
    John D. 5, 7, 13, 21, 59
    John F. 127, 138, 170
    Juanita 136

    Margaret 70
    Rick (Aka Mendocino Rick) xi, 25
Millville 15, 43, 95
Milton 73, 74, 80, 85, 113
Miner, Billy 108
Modoc County 56
Monroeville 90
Montgomery, A.W. 64
Montgomery Creek 102, 103
More, Marion 81
Morrow Grade 76, 112
Morrow, W.C. 161
Morse, Harry 152
Mountain Joe 9, 10, 11
Myers Grade 90

N

Navarro River 25
Nevada County 106, 171
Norris, Frank 171
Norton, Carol 6
Noyo River 58
Num-te-ra-re-man 82

O

Oak Run 14
Older, Fremont 171
Oldham, Sid 6
Old Shasta 4, 30, 31, 35, 37, 44
Ono 98
Oregon City xiii, 20, 23, 28, 58, 110
Oregon River 45
O'Reilly, Bill viii, 1, 72, 166, 171
Orophee (Oro Fino City) 109
Oroville 71, 92, 94, 103, 107
Orr, John 59
Owyhee County 81

P

Palace Hotel 44, 117, 118
Parrish
    Edward 28
    Merinda 28
Peanut 61, 167
Pehrson, N.J. 119
Pit River 12, 14, 28, 33, 35, 37, 43, 47, 48, 49, 50,
        51, 70, 71, 82, 94, 95, 102, 103, 107, 109,
        110, 122, 124, 138
Pit River Massacre 122

Pixley 135, 136
Placerville 23, 29, 61, 62, 65, 67, 68, 74, 101, 112, 114, 117, 118, 123, 125, 158, 159, 170
Point Arena 90, 97
Pope Valley 58, 109
Portland 81, 122
Portuguese Flat 32, 33
Potter Valley 26, 60

Q

Quincy 92

R

Reader
Frank 45, 88
Jim 44, 89
Reading's Grant 48
Red Bluff 14, 19, 20, 21, 28, 29, 32, 50, 61, 90
Redding x, 4, 23, 39, 86, 94, 95, 101, 102, 119, 184, 185, 186, 193
Reno 105, 116, 117, 158
Robertson
Alexander 118
Katie A. 97
Rocky Bar xiv, 9, 13, 15, 16, 17, 18, 19, 20, 21, 22, 23, 24, 26, 27, 58, 82, 98
Rogers 38, 49
Roman, Anton 37
Rosborough 37, 38, 49, 51, 159
Roseburg 5, 20, 101
Rosenus, Alan vii, 185
Round Mountain 14, 102, 103, 104
Round Valley 25, 183

S

Sacramento River 12, 21, 29, 32, 33, 35, 37, 48, 61, 101, 119, 124
Salisbury, Melinda xii
Salt Creek 35, 37, 138
San Andreas 131
San Diego 1, 57, 136, 160, 161, 170, 185
San Francisco 7, 10, 13, 19, 24, 25, 26, 37, 39, 44, 62, 65, 66, 67, 69, 72, 81, 82, 97, 107, 111, 114, 115, 116, 117, 118, 122, 123, 125, 127, 130, 133, 137, 138, 140, 144, 146, 159, 160, 161, 162, 167, 169, 181, 182, 183
San Hedren Mountain 111
San Joaquin Valley x, 135

San Quentin 26, 44, 57, 60, 62, 67, 108, 118, 121, 122, 123, 125, 126, 127, 133, 137, 148, 156, 159, 163, 170
Saratoga Springs 73
Schwartz, Lola Hawes 44
Scott Bar 38
Scott, Nelson 109
Scott River xiii, 38
Scott Valley xi, xiii, 4, 19, 21, 22, 23, 24, 31, 37, 40, 61, 66, 71, 83, 98, 99, 109
Sears, George 12
Shady Creek 88
Shasta, Calle 71
Shasta County x, 30, 82, 94, 100, 118, 167, 184
Shasta Lake 42, 94
Shasta Plains Township xiii
Shasta Valley 12, 33, 34, 41, 48, 119, 126, 171, 174
Sheep Rock 49
Sheridan 82
Shine, John 80
Sierra Nevada Mountains 111
Silver City 51, 70, 82
Silver Mountain 96
Simas, Jim xi, 4, 23
Siskiyou County xi, xiii, 4, 5, 13, 18, 23, 31, 33, 34, 71, 98, 100, 121, 138, 139, 185, 186
Sisson, Justin Hinckley 22, 167
Skillman, Archibald 37
Slate Creek 12, 119
Slicer, Hugh 162
Sluicer, John B. 47, 48
Smartsville 77, 80, 81, 106
Smith
Dottie 37, 102, 185
Nat xi, 17
Smithson, James 119
Soda Springs 33, 48, 101
Sonora 74, 80, 85, 113
Sontag x, 135
Southern, Mae Hazel x, 186
Squaw Flat 32
Squaw Mountain 33
Squaw Town 32
Squaw Valley 12, 33, 49, 139
Stevenson, James 49
Stoddard, Charles Warren 68, 83, 124
Summit Valley 26
Sunny Ridge 33
Sutter 21, 28

T

Tadpole Miners 32
Tauhindali, Bill (Towendolly) 33
Texas Springs 32
Thorn 114
Timber Cove 59
Tompkins, Frank 109
Tower House 31, 98
Trinity River 38, 53, 177
Two Rock 91

U

Ukiah xi, 25, 26, 27, 60, 64, 92, 93, 106
Umpqua Valley 5

V

Visalia 135
Vollmers, Eric xii, 171

W

Wabash 6, 175, 181
Walker, William 32
Walla Walla 6, 13, 14
Warner, Charles Dudley 136
Watkins
    Frank x, xii, 12, 13, 14, 15, 16, 17, 18, 19, 20,
        24, 25, 26, 27, 28, 29, 30, 33, 37, 41, 44,
        45, 58, 60, 61, 62, 63, 64, 73, 88, 95, 98,
        100, 103, 104, 108, 109, 111, 124, 137,
        148, 161, 171, 183, 184
    Greg 44, 45, 88, 118
    Ursula 44
Weaverville 61, 174, 176
Webb House 44, 117
Weed 48, 167
Wells
    Harry L (H.L.W) xi, xiii, 4, 5, 11, 12, 20, 23,
        28, 30, 31, 34, 98, 100, 109, 121, 123,
        125, 138, 171, 186
    Hudson 11, 12
Wells Fargo viii, xiv, 72, 97, 117, 131, 135,
    157, 166
White's Ranch 62
Wilcox, Ella Wheeler 124, 125
Wilde
    C.K.W 161
    Oscar 83, 161
Willamette Valley 83

Williams, Horace 101, 107
Willitsville 106
Wintu Indians xi, 35, 70, 164, 193
Wright, Ben 30, 40, 167

Y

Yana 43
Yreka xiii, xiv, 6, 7, 9, 16, 18, 19, 21, 22, 30, 31, 34,
    35, 37, 38, 39, 40, 41, 42, 48, 49, 50, 53, 59,
    66, 69, 71, 75, 82, 83, 84, 86, 87, 90, 97, 98,
    99, 100, 101, 110, 111, 122, 123, 124, 126,
    139, 157, 158, 159, 170, 174
Yreka Creek 38, 40, 53, 123, 126
Yuba 80, 81
Yuki 43

Z

Zornes, Arlene xi

About the Author

Margaret Guilford-Kardell (1920-) has a B.S. in Agricultural Economics from U. C .Berkeley (1942) and an M.S. also in Ag. Econ. from the Univ. of Tenn. (1943). She drove a jeep and a truck as a WWII Volunteer in the U.S. Coast Guard Port Security Force, while back in Oakland CA, before more research assistant work at U.C. Davis and abroad. As a teenager she lived in Oakland, CA and walked to Joaquin Miller park, did high school in Merced, CA traveled worldwide, living in seven different countries. She retired first to the McCloud River area in CA and finally moved to Blaine, WA. Some publications by Margaret Guilford-Kardell include; The Occasional Papers of Redding California, Autobiography on the Life, Times, and Exploits of Cininnatus Hiner Miller, The Joaquin Miller Newsletters, many articles for the Californian, and various articles on Wintu Indians. Google Margaret Kardell or Margaret Guilford-Kardell for more publications and articles.

Printed in the United States
By Bookmasters